The SIERRA CLUB Guide to 35 mm Landscape Photography

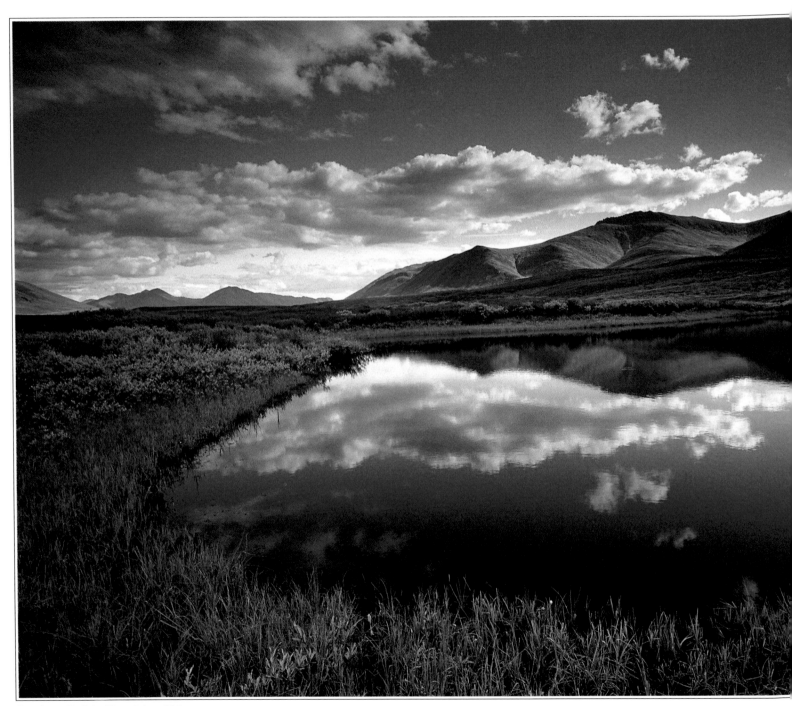

Southern Ogilvie Mountains, Yukon

The SIERRA CLUB Guide
to 35 mm Landscape Photography

Text and Photos by
Tim Fitzharris

Sierra Club Books San Francisco

LIBRARY OF CONGRESS CATALOGING-IN-PUBLICATION DATA

Fitzharris, Tim, 1948-
   The Sierra Club Guide to 35 mm Landscape Photography / by Tim Fitzharris
      p. cm.
   ISBN 0-87156-404-1
   1. Landscape photography—Handbooks, manuals, etc. 2. 35 mm cameras. I. Sierra Club. II. Title
   TR660.F58 1994   94-1469
   778.9'36—dc20   CIP

Produced by Terrapin Books, Santa Fe, New Mexico

Printed in Hong Kong

10 9 8 7 6 5 4 3 2

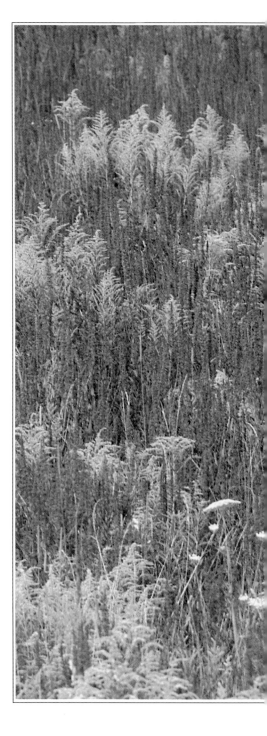

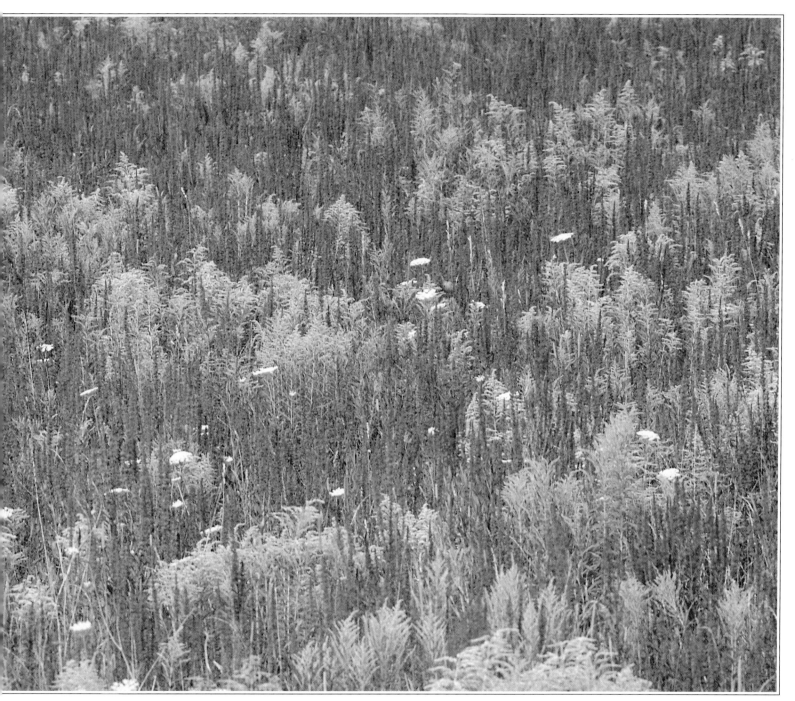

Purple Loosestrife, Queen Anne's Lace, and Goldenrod Meadow, Perth, Ontario

FOR JOY

Books by Tim Fitzharris

The Adventure of Nature Photography

The Island

The Wild Prairie

Wildflowers of Canada (with Audrey Fraggalosch)

British Columbia Wild

Canada: A Natural History (with John Livingston)

Wild Birds of Canada

Forest: A National Audubon Society Book

The Audubon Society Guide to Nature Photography

Wild Wings: An Introduction to Birdwatching

Coastal Wildlife of British Columbia (with Bruce Obee)

Soaring with Ravens

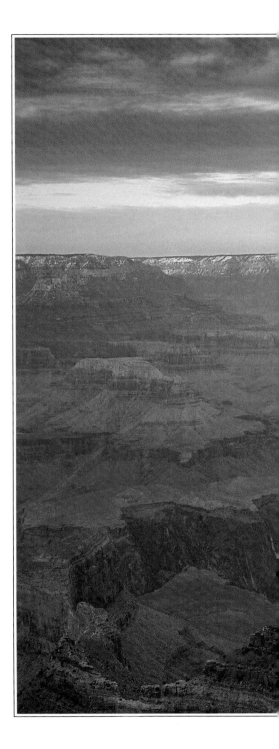

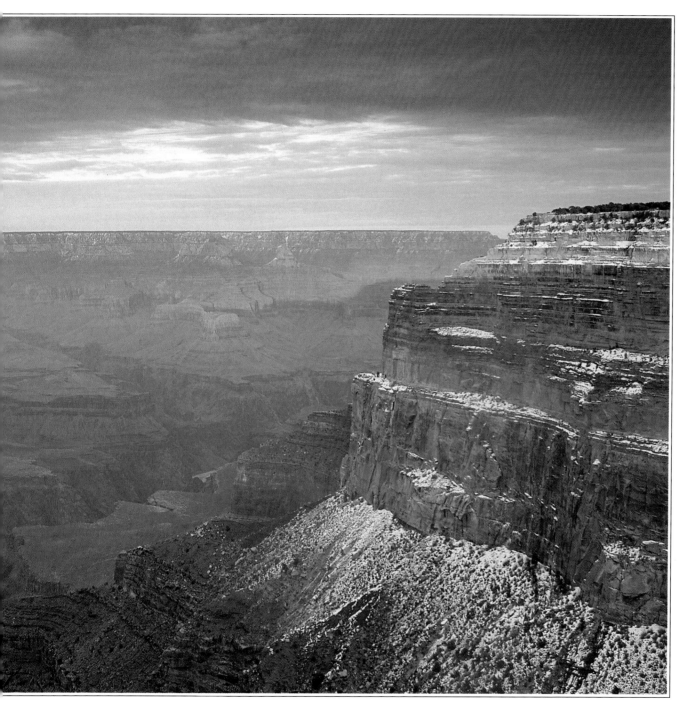

South Rim, Grand Canyon, Arizona

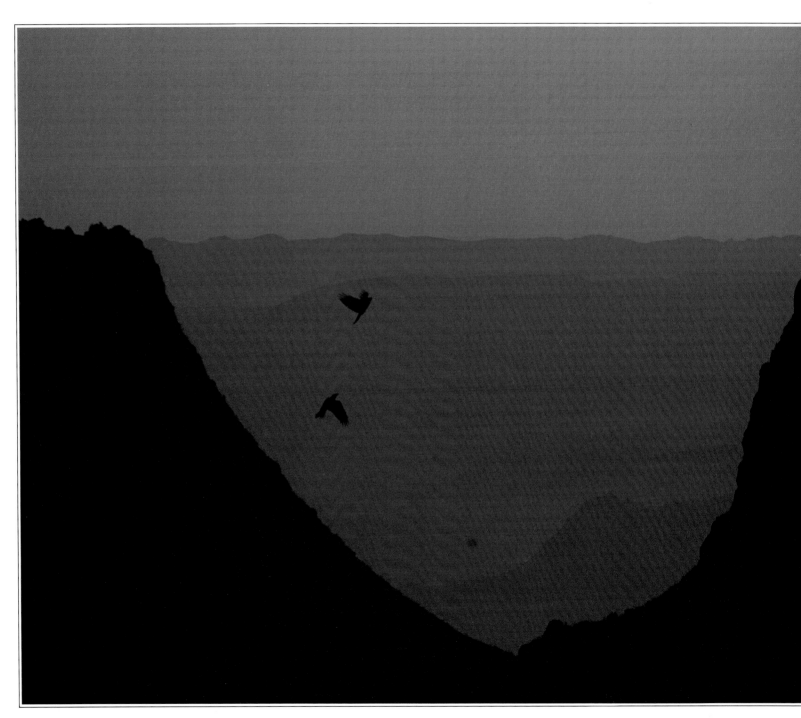

The Window, Big Bend National Park, Texas

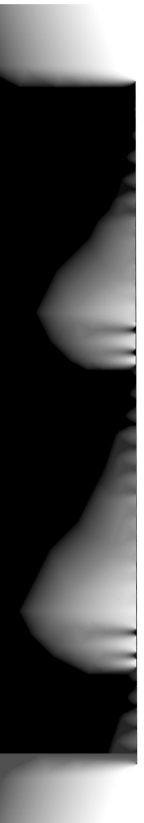

CONTENTS

Introduction

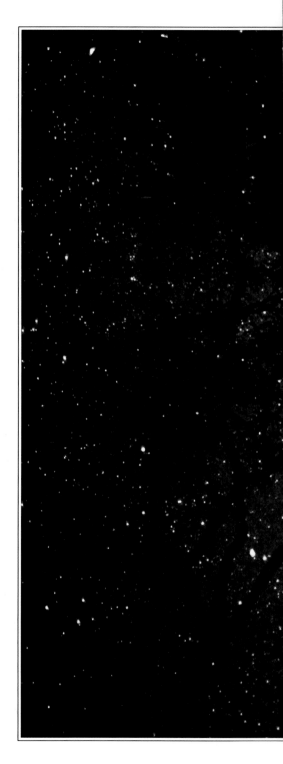

EXCEPTIONAL PHOTOGRAPHS of the landscape are seldom the result of luck, seldom the result of a snapshot made while hiking a mountain trail. For the landscape photographer, pressing the shutter button is almost an afterthought, the last step in a process of study, research, exploration, and artistic insight.

More than anything else, scenic photography requires that you be able to control the effect that light has on the landscape. You need to become aware of the different properties of light—its color, direction, intensity, and texture. And you must know how these properties react with film in the creation of a photograph. Color is the most important component of the landscape, and together with light, it is the most important consideration when designing a picture.

Although this book deals with 35 mm scenic photography, its advice is useful to the users of any camera format. Until recently, many picture editors and photography critics felt that landscape photographs were best made by larger cameras because of the fine detail they rendered. However, for most publications—books, magazines, postcards, calendars—fine-grained 35 mm transparency films can deliver more detail

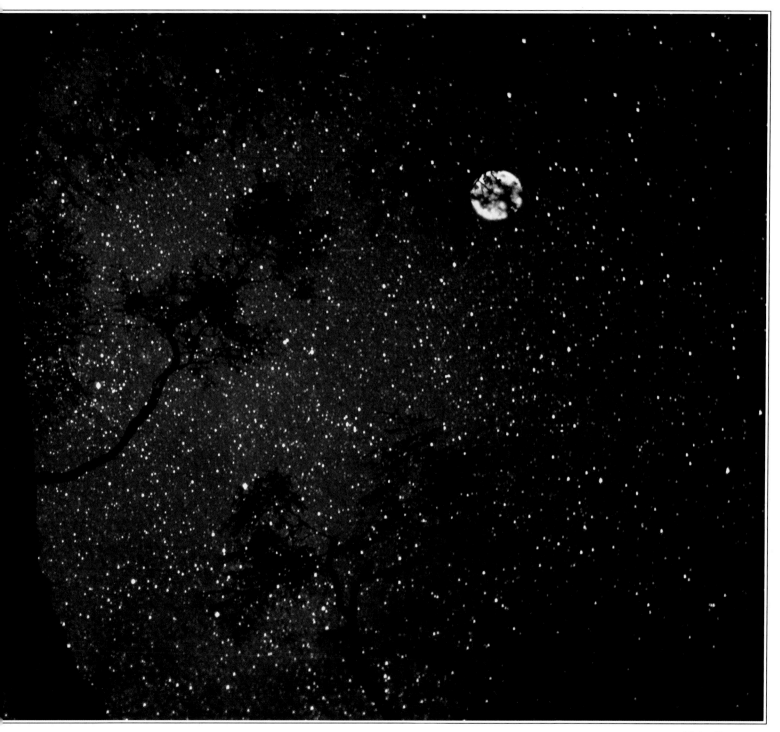

Night Skyscape

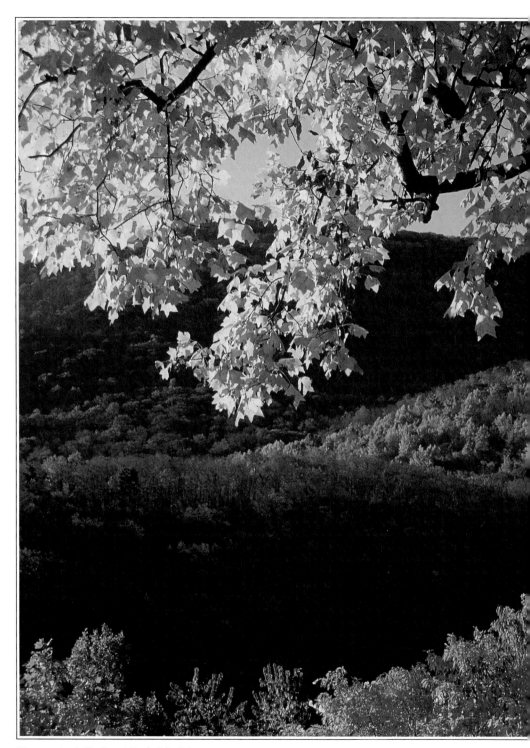

Shenandoah National Park, Virginia

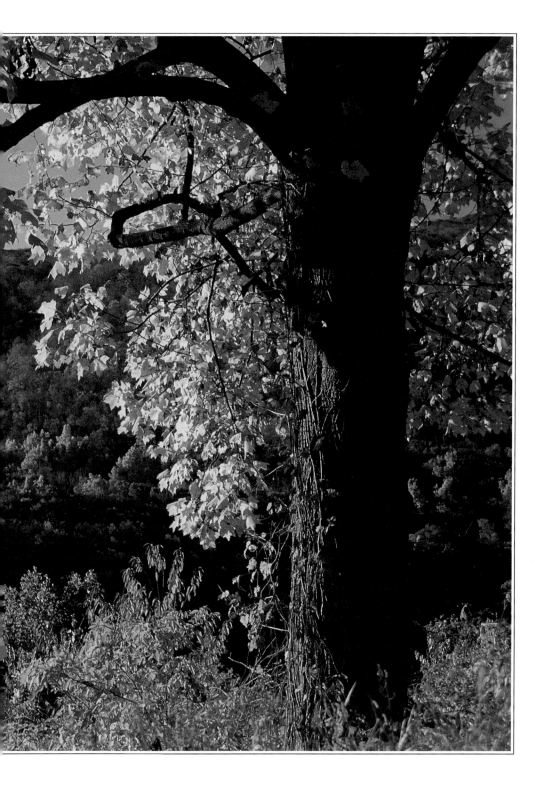

than the human eye can see. And 35 mm cameras have many practical advantages over larger formats. They are lighter, easier to handle, offer greater technical control, and are less expensive to purchase and operate. They allow the photographer to work with greater freedom, spontaneity and creativity.

Landscape photography differs little technically from other fields of photography. Its challenge is to express a unique visual perception. To do this, you should have a thorough understanding and control of the medium; you should understand the psychology of human vision as it relates to two-dimensional design; and you should understand the essential nature of the subject, especially as it affects you personally. At some point in your development as a photographer, the logic of these fundamental considerations gives way to intuition, and it is usually then that you express yourself with the most clarity and power.

PART I

Equipment

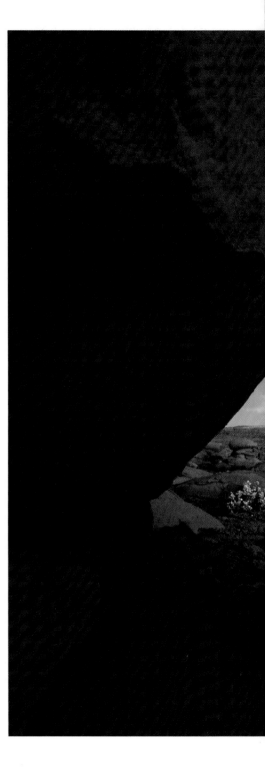

THE EQUIPMENT REQUIRED for scenic photography is not specialized. You need a camera, tripod, lenses, filters, and carrying bag.

CAMERA

Even though there are hundreds of 35 mm camera models in existence, it is not difficult to decide which ones are suitable for landscape photography. Such cameras can also be used for other nature subjects, including wildlife. There are two basic types of 35 mm cameras, the rangefinder and the single-lens-reflex (SLR). Rangefinder cameras are inadequate for professional calibre landscape photography. They have two separate lenses, one for viewing the scene and the other for directing light onto the film. What you see is different, especially at close range, from what actually appears in the photograph. Further, rangefinder cameras allow limited, or no, lens interchange. The single-lens-reflex camera has none of these drawbacks. The scene is

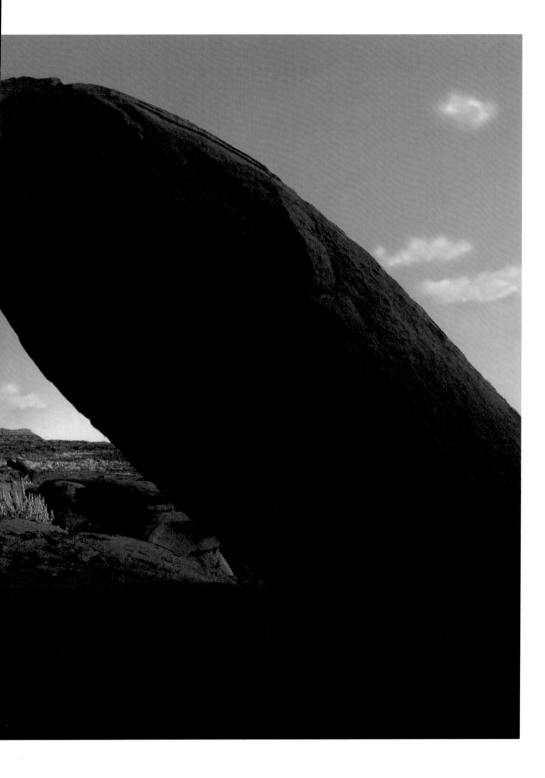

Painted Desert, Arizona. *The rocks in the foreground of this picture could easily be picked up with one hand. I arranged them in order to make a window that would frame the distant scene.The camera was placed on the ground in front of the window, using small pebbles to support the lens. I lay down to make the final framing adjustments with my eye to the viewfinder. The entire process took only five or ten minutes thanks to the easy-handling 35 mm SLR camera that I was using. The shot would have been almost impossible to make using any other camera format.*

15

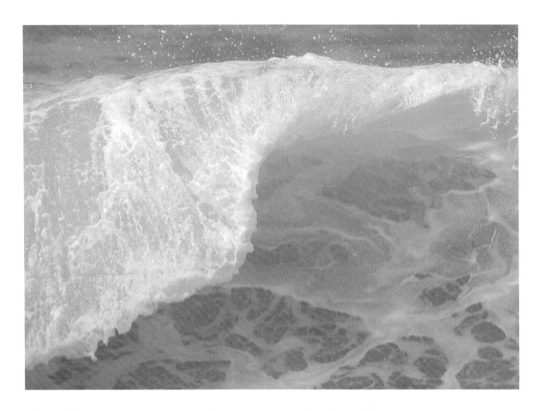

Wave at Bonzai Beach, Oahu. *Several specialized features of the 35 mm SLR were important in making this photograph. The viewfinder's accurate, uninterrupted framing of the scene allowed me to compose the picture quickly and trip the shutter just as the wave was breaking. A 500 mm telephoto lens permitted a close-up view, yet allowed me to shoot from dry land where the camera was safe from spray and occasional high-breaking waves.*

Waimea Bay, Oahu. *This scene is in focus from the rocks in the foreground to the clouds in the distance. The waves are blurred because of a slow shutter speed (2 seconds). In most landscape photographs, it is desirable to have all of the scene in focus. A depth-of-field preview lever permits you to view the scene at the shooting aperture, as it will be portrayed in the final photograph.*

viewed directly through the lens by means of a short periscope, called a pentaprism. Just prior to exposure, a mirror that reflects the image up through the pentaprism to your eye swings out of the way, allowing light to strike the film. The mirror returns so quickly that the photographer's view of the scene is essentially uninterrupted. The body of the single-lens-reflex camera is the nucleus of an extensive system of accessories, the most important ones being interchangeable lenses.

BUYING AN SLR CAMERA

There are many excellent brands of SLR cameras, but four dominate the market and are recommended: Nikon, Minolta, Canon, and Pentax. Nikon equipment is generally the most expensive, but not necessarily the best. I have used Canon cameras for many years, but I would be happy with any of the other systems. Buy the camera body only, unless it comes with one of the lenses recommended later in the chapter. When you buy a camera, make sure it has the following features. (Other important features, such as lens interchange, are not mentioned because they are standard on almost every SLR.)

Depth-of-field preview. This mechanism provides a preview of the scene at shooting aperture, a procedure that allows you to determine how much of the image will be in focus in the final photograph. This may be different from

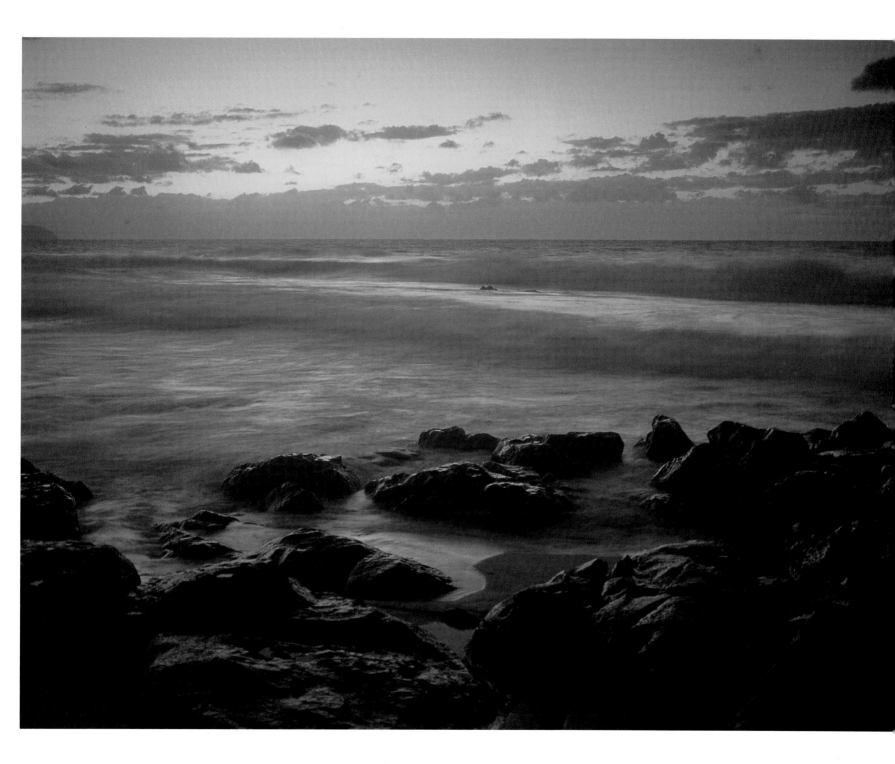

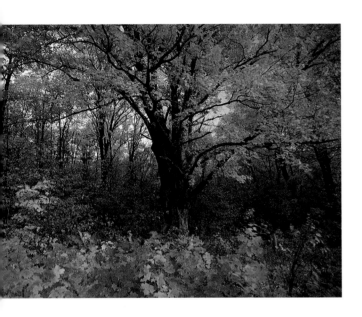

Sugar Maple Forest, Gatineau Park, Quebec.
A variable pattern light-meter allows you to select
how the light reflected from the scene will be
measured. With this photograph, there is little
variation of brightness throughout the scene. As a
result, any metering pattern will produce the
same exposure. I based this exposure on an average reading of the entire scene.

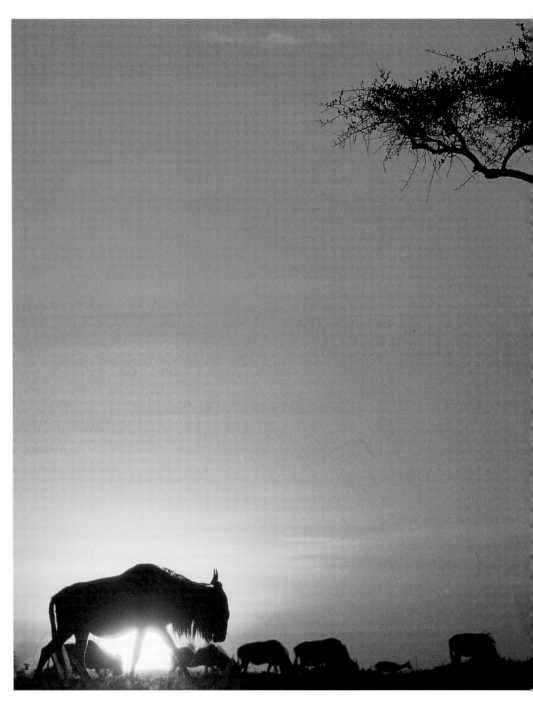

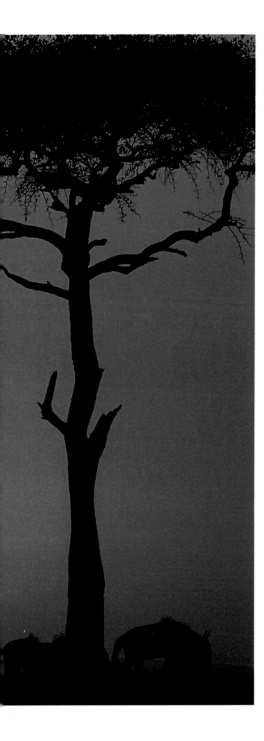

what is shown in the viewfinder. Make sure that this switch is conveniently placed, as you will be using it almost every time you take a picture.

Manual exposure control. Most new cameras have automatic exposure control. Make sure you are able to turn off this feature and control exposure manually.

Variable-pattern light meter. This provides a choice of light measuring patterns. Although some cameras offer five or six different patterns, it is sufficient to have just three—full screen averaging, center-weighted, and spot metering.

The following features are not necessary, but they make shooting more convenient.

Automatic film advance. This is valuable when you wish to make a series of identical photographs. Manual film advance can easily jar the camera and throw off precise framing even if the camera is mounted on a tripod.

Automatic film indexing. The light meter is automatically programmed for the speed of the film in use. It's easy to forget to reset the film speed should you switch film types.

AUTO-FOCUS CAMERAS

Automatic focusing is not desirable for scenic photography (or even wildlife photography), but nearly all new cameras have this feature. Camera manufacturers continually revise the designs of

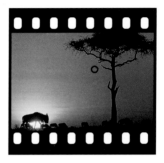

Wildebeest at Sunrise, Kenya. *At sunrise or sunset, the brightness of the scene varies greatly, especially if the sun is included in the composition. In order to preserve the rich color of the sky in this scene, I based the exposure on a spot-meter reading of a portion of the sky that I wished to be rendered accurately (shown inside circle). This caused underexposure in the foreground elements, rendering them as silhouettes, and overexposure of the sun. Motor-driven film advance made it possible to take several pictures as the wildebeest passed in front of the sun. I picked the best frame once the film was developed.*

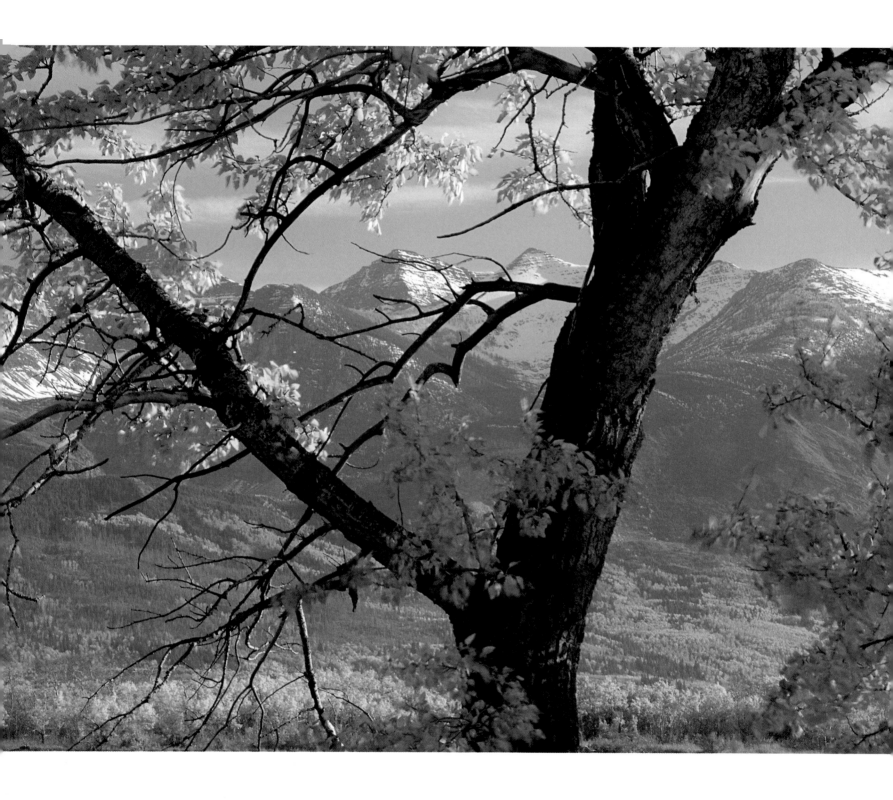

their products to stimulate sales. As a result they add many features that seem advantageous in theory, but perform poorly in practice. Auto-focusing is one of them. You can turn it off, but unfortunately, you still have to pay for the extra technology, added weight, and increased battery drain.

MAIL ORDER CAMERAS

This is the least expensive way to buy a camera, and to my mind, the best. You may think that the advice you get from your local camera store is worth the extra money that the store charges for the equipment, but you are just as likely to get misleading information because the staff is not well trained or has little practical experience. It is better to learn what equipment will serve you best by studying magazines and books.

The best source of mail order camera suppliers is found in the back pages of *Popular Photography* magazine.

Glacier-Waterton Lakes International Park, Montana/Alberta. *As a site for landscape photography, this park offers many lakes for reflected views, no crowds, inspiring mountain scenery, and abundant wildlife.*

Schwabacher Landing, Grand Teton National Park, Wyoming. *Like most reflected views, this classic scene is best photographed in the early morning when the ponds are most likely to be still.*

📷 ON LOCATION *SCENIC HOTSPOT*

WHEN TRAVELLING to a new location for photography, I first familiarize myself with the potential of the area. I visit local bookstores (visitor centers in national parks) to browse through souvenir picture books, postcards, and calendars, and make notes of shooting sites. I make a tour of the area to get an idea of how the landscape will be lit throughout the day, particularly at dawn and dusk. Once I know the logistic requirements, and have an extended weather forecast, I can work out a loose shooting schedule for my visit.

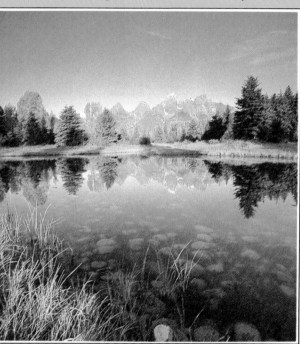

Each location has famous, often photographed views that I shoot first, such as the Grand Tetons from Schwabacher Landing, Turret Arch through North Arch at Arches National Park, or Bryce Canyon from Inspiration Point. Then I start shooting with a more personal approach, trying for something unusual. I plan on recording one scenic feature for each sunrise and sunset period. During the day, I check new sites to determine where I will set up the tripod once the light is right.

My schedule is dependent on the weather. If it is overcast, I switch from shooting landforms in low light to shooting vegetation patterns during midday. If there is a storm, I try to shoot through the bad weather in hopes of capturing some dramatic effects. When working, I discipline myself to setup only on scenes with outstanding merit. This goal makes the process more exciting and the results more worthwhile. Scenic areas abound in North America. In addition to the ones described in this book, California's Big Sur, the Oregon Coast, Glacier National Park, Hawaii's Na Pali Coast, Monument Valley, Canyonlands National Park, and Vermont's Green Mountains are among my favorites.

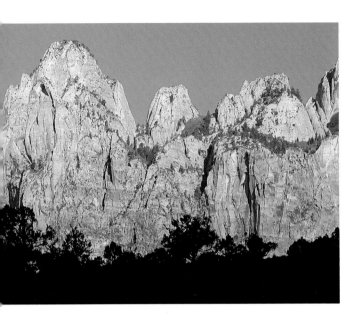

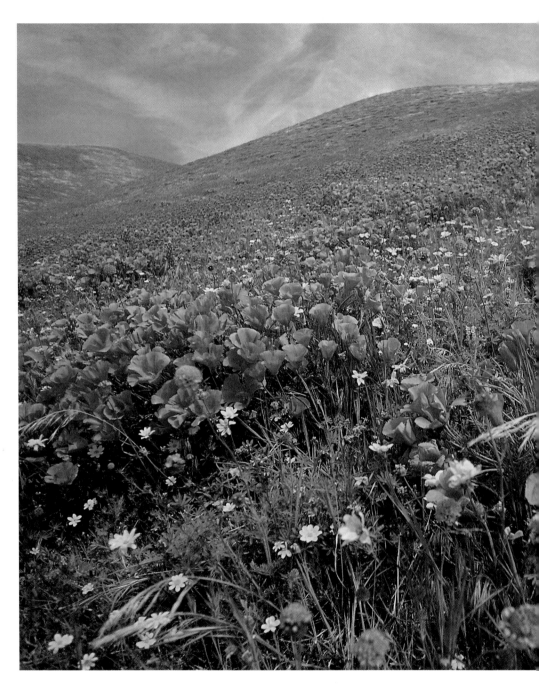

Towers of the Virgin, Zion National Park, Utah.
These peaks were photographed with a 70 mm—
300 mm zoom lens at its maximum focal length.
The telephoto perspective enlarges the scene,
and more importantly, flattens perspective.

Poppy Meadows, Antelope Valley, California.
Lens focal length affects the way perspective is
rendered. The 18 mm lens used here spreads out
picture elements, making the flowers in the foreground appear farther away from the distant hills.

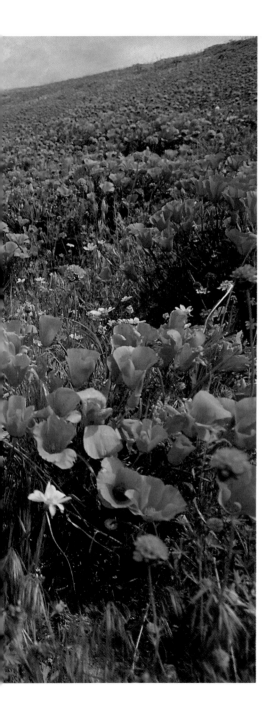

USED CAMERAS

An older model manual camera is an excellent purchase provided it meets the criteria described above. Many of these older models have excellent features, quality workmanship, and none of the extraneous technology that makes many modern cameras difficult to use. The better the camera looks on the outside (a few scratches and dents are seldom a problem), the better it will be on the inside. If possible, have the camera's shutter speeds, light meter, and lens mechanisms checked by a repair shop before you buy. The fee should be around $20, or nothing if you are buying it from a retailer that has a repair facility on the premises.

LENSES

The specification of a lens usually consists of two measurements: the magnifying power of the lens (the focal length) is measured in millimeters and its light gathering power (the maximum aperture) is designated by an f/number. A telephoto lens (over 50 mm) magnifies the subject and a wide-angle lens (less than 50 mm) makes it smaller, providing a wider view. The smaller the f/number, the larger is the maximum aperture of the lens.

Lenses with large apertures are called 'fast' lenses because they allow the use of fast shutter speeds. Fast lenses are expensive. In landscape photography, their larger size and weight is a handicap. They will tax your stamina and patience, and in the final analysis reduce the number of good pictures you take. Lens speed is useful primarily when shooting action.

LENSES YOU SHOULD HAVE

The ideal range of lenses includes focal lengths from 17 or 18 mm to 300 mm. Zoom lenses provide many different focal lengths in one barrel. By zooming in or out on the scene, the photographer achieves precise framing without having to change the camera position. For adequate optical quality, be sure to buy zoom lenses that have glass elements described as 'APO', 'ED', 'Extra-low Dispersion', or 'Aspherical'. These designations mean that the lens uses high quality glass elements which eliminate the unwanted distortion inherent in standard zoom lenses. The front element of the lens should not retract into the barrel when zooming or focusing. This prevents the use of certain essential filters and filter-holders.

17 mm or 18 mm wide-angle, f/4 or faster. Make sure that you are able to attach filters to the front of the lens. (Some ultra-wide-angle lenses have built-in lens hoods or protruding front elements that prevent front filter attachment.)

20 mm—70 mm zoom, f/4 or faster. Most of your pictures will be taken with this lens.

80 mm—300 mm zoom, f/5.6 or faster. Anything similar to this will work. High ratio zoom lenses can be of poor optical quality unless special glass

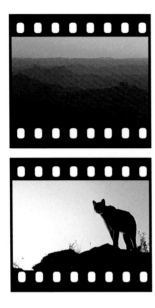

Canyonlands National Park, Utah. *Like most scenic photographs, this one would not have been possible without a tripod. Taken in the weak light before sunrise, the long exposure (eight seconds) made hand-holding impossible. In addition, I used a 200 mm focal length which multiplies any camera movement that occurs during exposure to the same degree that it magnifies the scene (four times). The mountain lion was photographed separately and added to the composition by sandwiching the two slides together.*

elements (see above) are used in the design.

Lenses made by independent manufacturers, such as Sigma, Tamron, or Tokina, are less expensive than camera-brand lenses, of equal quality, and sometimes better design.

TRIPODS

Nearly all landscape photography is done with a tripod-mounted camera. Plan to spend as much on a tripod as you would for a telephoto zoom lens. Be sure that the tripod you buy has the following features.

1) lightweight, aluminum, 3 section tubular legs.

2) lever or clip lock legs (avoid collar locks which jam easily when the tripod is used in dusty or wet conditions).

3) legs without center braces so that the legs can be spread at different widths, a frequent necessity on uneven ground.

4) an extended height that brings the camera close to eye level when the center column is not elevated.

5) a heavy duty ball and socket head with a quick release platform (allowing the camera to be quickly mounted and unmounted).

A tripod that satisfies all of these requirements is the Bogen 3021 with the Bogen ballhead 3055. A lot of photographers use Foba or Swiss Arca heads that are much heavier and cost as much as six times more than the Bogen 3055. In addition to the extra cost, these heads are very heavy. The degree of stability they provide is

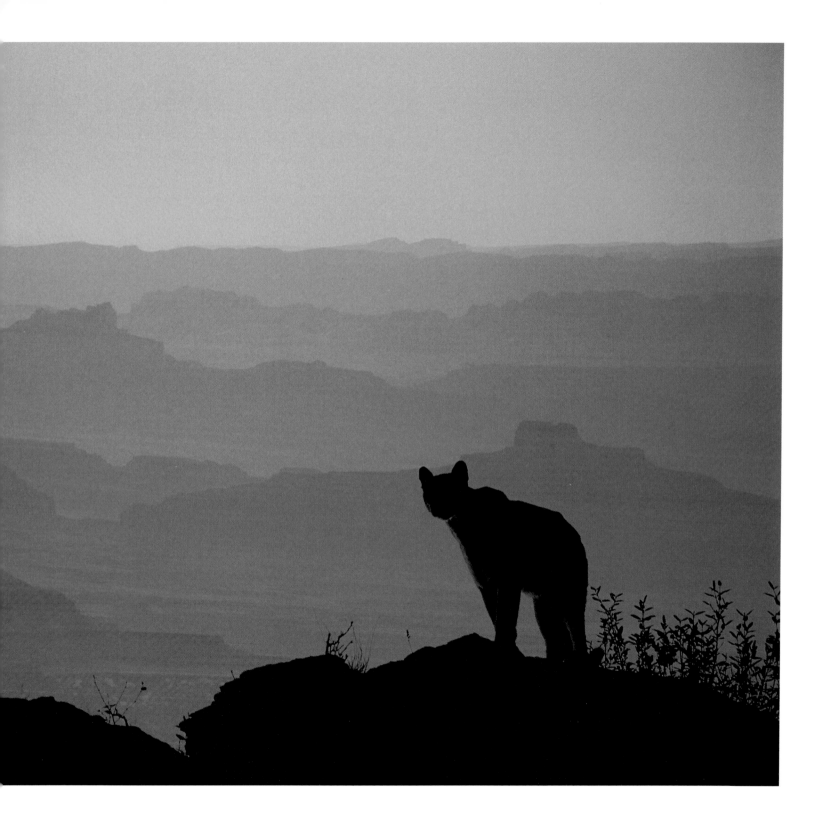

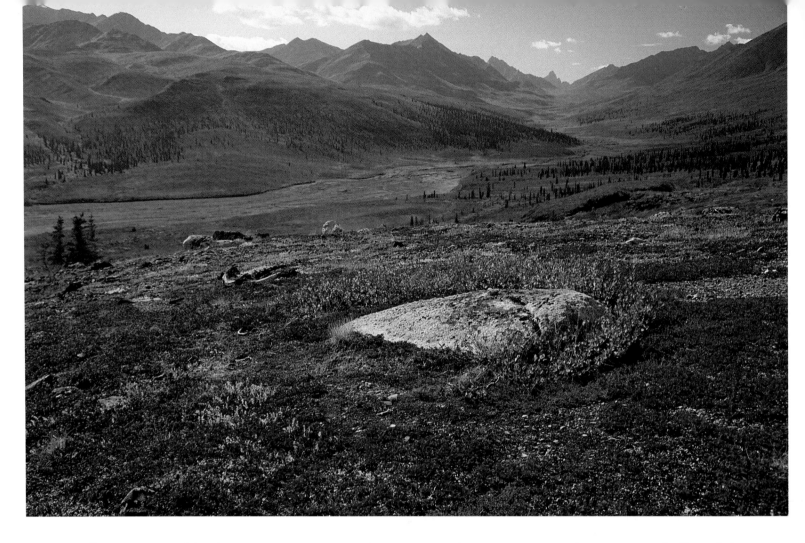

unnecessary. If you must get one of these heavy-weights, the Bogan Pro Art head is a good choice. It's the same weight and quality as the designer brands, but half the price.

The Bogen clamp is a useful tripod accessory which fastens securely to the bottom of a tripod leg and provides a mount for a ball and socket head. This is the best way to position the camera close to, or at, ground level. The conventional procedure is to reverse the center column and hang the camera between the tripod legs. However, with this technique, the camera is not adequately stable, access to the viewfinder is blocked by the tripod legs, and the camera controls, being upside-down, are difficult to operate.

CAMERA BAGS

Bags alone are not heavy, so get the biggest one you can afford. If all your camera equipment doesn't fill it up, wait awhile. In the meantime, you have extra storage for film, trailmix, sunscreen and your wallet. Make sure the bag is waterproof, made of ballistic materials, and has adjustable interior dividers. Lowepro and Tamrac produce the industry standard for top quality bags. They are expensive (about the price of a telephoto lens) but they will normally last a lifetime.

I like to use a regular shoulder bag because it allows the quickest access to equipment. However,

26

📷 DEMPSTER HIGHWAY *SCENIC HOTSPOT*

IN ALL THE vast wild country of Alaska and northern Canada, only one public road, the Dempster Highway, reaches into the sub-artic tundra to cross the Arctic Circle. This strip of gravel stretches 460 miles from Dawson City to Inuvik on the Mackenzie River delta. The highway is above treeline for most of its length, affording views of nothing but wilderness for a hundred miles in every direction. It crosses a dozen rivers and penetrates three mountain ranges. Here, great herds of caribou pass the winter beneath the northern lights, grizzlies dig for ground squirrels, loons sing from shallow lakes, and wildflowers enliven the tundra in summer. For me the Dempster holds one singular attraction; for there are places where wildlife is more abundant and mountain ranges more dramatic. Not even in the Green Mountains of Vermont is autumn more beautiful. During the last two weeks of August, the frost-nipped tundra is set ablaze by the scarlet leaves of kinnickinnick and huckleberry and the gold of dwarf willow and birch. In the region of the Ogilvie Mountains, the rolling terrain is painted deep red from horizon to horizon, presenting one breathtaking vista after another.

The staging area for this arctic adventure is Dawson City. Once you leave town, there are no services of any kind along the highway. You have to camp and carry enough food and gasoline to either get back to Dawson City or travel onward to Inuvik. During a full day on the road, you will see only another car or two, so be prepared for emergencies. For more information, write Department of Tourism, Dept. 7227, Box 2703, Whitehorse, Yukon, Canada Y1A 2C8.

Eagle Flats, Yukon. No public road in North America is as remote as the Dempster Highway (see inset) from which this photo was taken. When working in such out-of-the-way places, I guard against equipment failure by carrying an extra camera body, tripod head, and spare parts for my tripod legs. In addition, I keep a set of jewellers screw drivers in my camera bag to tighten screws loosened by travel on rough roads, such as the Dempster.

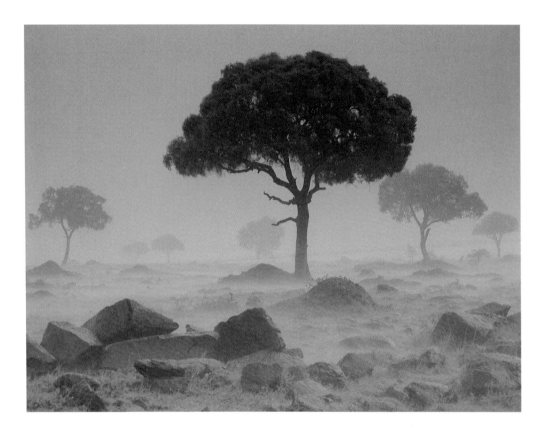

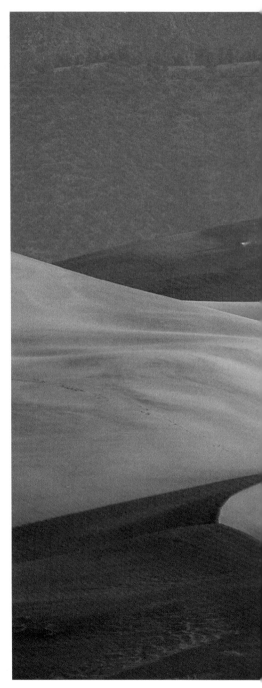

Rainstorm, Serengeti Plains, Kenya. *I photographed this torrential downpour with the camera mounted on a tripod set up inside the jeep that I was driving. My biggest problem was positioning the jeep so that the acacia trees presented the most pleasing arrangement and yet keep the open window through which I was shooting to leeward, so that water was not blown onto the camera.*

Great Sand Dunes National Monument, Colorado. *Few scenic elements are more attractive than the graceful shapes and satin textures of sand dunes. Unfortunately, working in such locations can disable cameras and lenses should sand particles get into interior mechanisms. I keep my camera bag closed when it is on the ground to avoid kicking sand inside. Should a part become jammed, forcing it will usually result in further damage. The only remedy is usually professional disassembly and cleaning.*

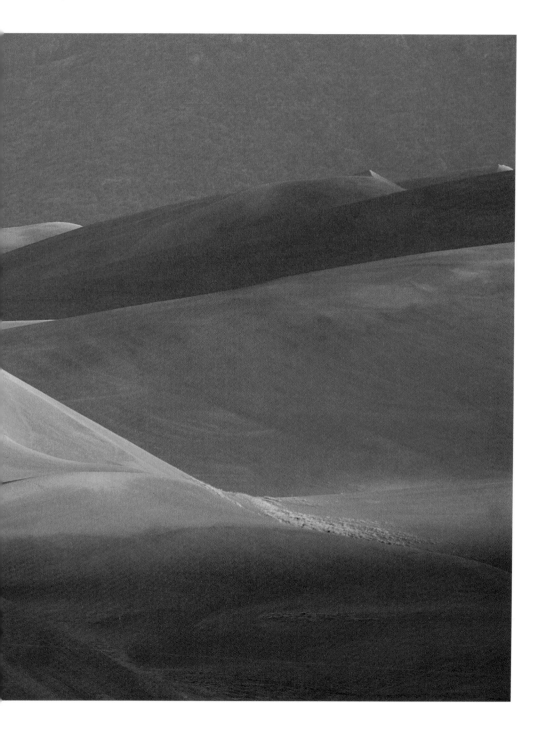

if you do a lot of hiking, get a bag that is worn like a backpack. Hard cases provide more protection, but they are not as easy to carry, nor as convenient to work from. All but the largest of the backpack bags can be taken aboard aircraft as carry-on luggage.

CARE OF EQUIPMENT

About the only thing that will harm your equipment is moisture, and of course, dropping it into the Grand Canyon. If your camera should get wet, dry it off and get it into a warm, dry air stream long enough to vaporize any of the moisture that might have seeped into the interior. Without opening up the camera, you can only guess how long this might take, so err on the safe side. If I have to shoot in the rain or snow, I work under a big umbrella held by an assistant.

Keep your equipment as clean as possible to prevent grime from working its way into the camera and gumming up delicate mechanisms. Open the camera back and brush out the film chamber regularly to prevent accumulating particles from scratching the film emulsion during transport. Be careful not to touch the shutter curtains themselves. In cold weather, batteries, especially alkaline types, are quickly exhausted. Keep a spare set warm in your pocket and switch the two sets in and out as needed.

PART II

Light and Film

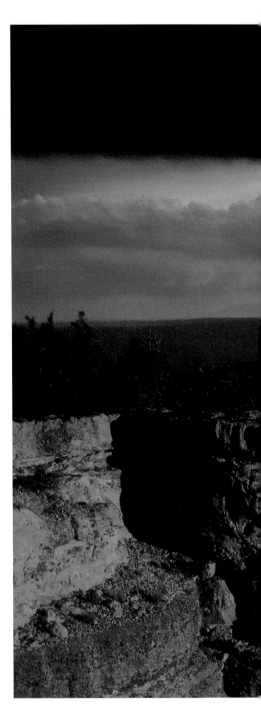

LIGHT IS THE essence of photography. A change in the way it illuminates the land can transform a commonplace scene into one of high drama. Four properties of light are important—intensity, direction, color, and texture.

LIGHT INTENSITY AND EXPOSURE

A film's sensitivity to light remains constant while the intensity of the sun's light changes during the day. By making adjustments to the camera's shutter speed and lens aperture, you can regulate the amount of light reaching the film and achieve proper exposure.

The lens aperture controls the light's intensity—the larger the aperture, the greater the intensity. Aperture settings, called f/stops, are commonly calibrated as f/2, f/2.8, f/4, f/5.6, f/8, f/11, and f/16. Larger numbers represent smaller apertures. Each aperture setting is one-half the size of the next larger one.

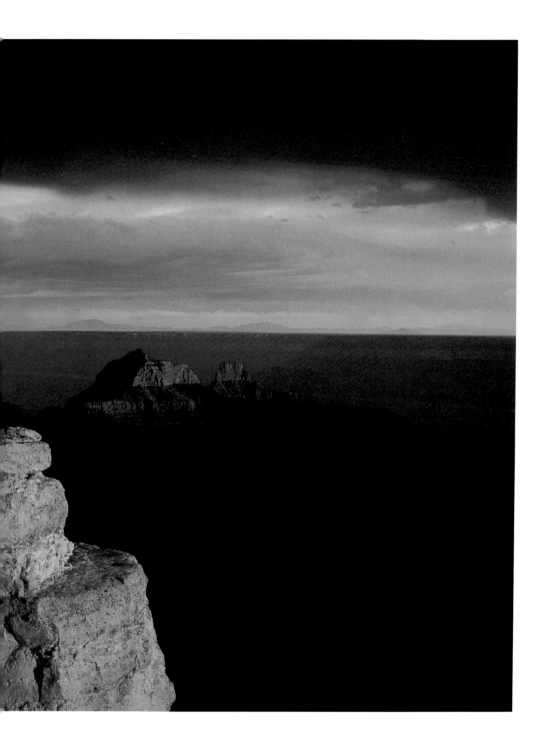

North Rim of the Grand Canyon, Arizona. As with most dramatic photos, light is the key element in this picture. It strikes the scene from the back and side, outlining rock contours and illuminating surface relief. Filtered by atmospheric particles, light bathes the rocks in a warm glow, typical of sunrise or sunset. Its low angle throws the lower canyon into shadow which provides effective contrast to the spotlit formations of the rim.

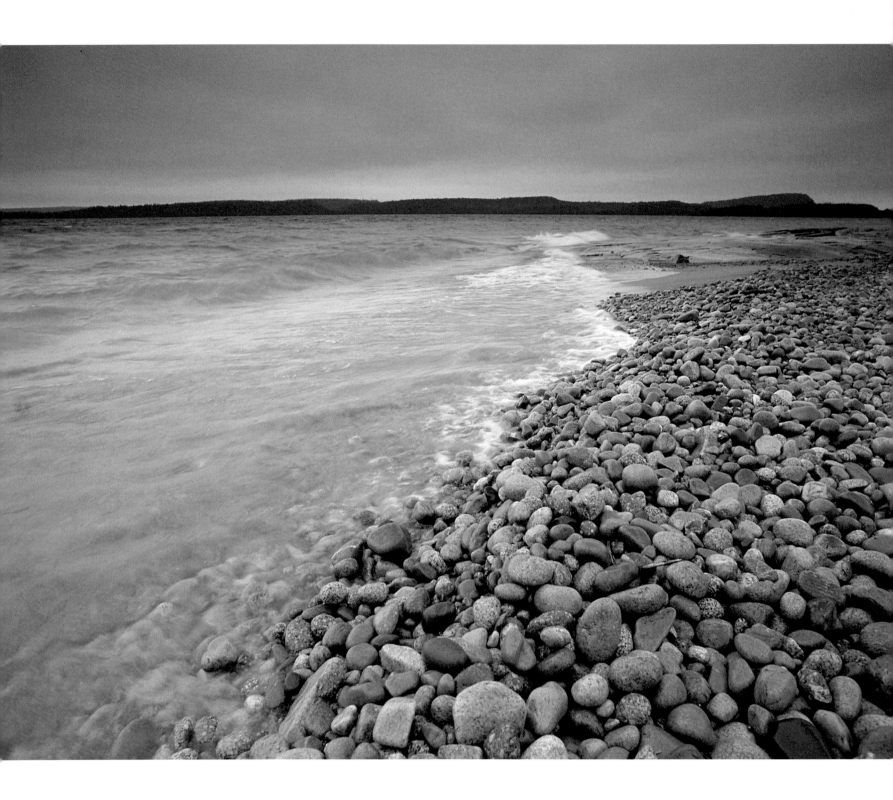

The shutter controls the duration of the exposure. The longer the exposure, the greater is the intensity of light striking the film. Exposure times are calibrated so that each setting is halved with every increase in shutter speed. Standard speeds in seconds are 1, 1/2, 1/4, 1/8, 1/15, 1/30, 1/60, 1/125, 1/250, 1/500, 1/1000, and faster.

In order to set the aperture and shutter speed, you must first measure the light reflected from the scene using the camera's built-in light meter. The meter will indicate a combination of f/stop and shutter speed needed for correct exposure. You then make the appropriate settings. With an auto-exposure camera, this is done for you.

Aside from controlling exposure, aperture and shutter speed affect picture design (discussed in the next chapter). As a result you may wish to alter the settings from those indicated by the light meter. Fortunately, aperture and shutter speed settings are reciprocal. If wish to use a larger aperture, simply select a correspondingly smaller (more brief) shutter speed, and proper exposure will be maintained.

Light meters are designed to read every scene as if it were average. They are unreliable when confronted with an abnormal situation. If the scene is a mixture of varied colors, with no dominance of bright or dark hues, then you follow the reading of the meter. Auto-exposure cameras work fine in such situations. Difficulties arise when the scene is not average—snow and beach

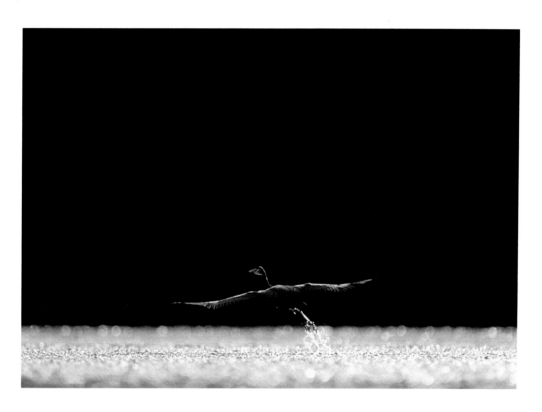

North Shore, Lake Superior, Ontario. *For most scenes, there are several combinations of aperture and shutter speed that you can choose for correct exposure. In order to attain the greatest depth-of-field (zone of sharpness) in this picture, a small aperture was chosen. As a result, a relatively long shutter speed was needed.*

Great Blue Heron, Vancouver Island. *To freeze the motion of the heron and splashing water, a fast shutter speed was called for. I underexposed two stops from the meter reading to retain the dark color of the water and background.*

scenes, spotlit or backlit landscapes, scenes dominated by a single light or dark color. If you follow the meter reading, the unusual brightness or darkness, so important to the scene, will be lost. The brilliant color of an autumn aspen grove will be muddied by inadequate exposure, fields of snow will be reproduced as gray, and spotlit subjects will be washed-out by overexposure.

It is easy to compensate for the meter's failings. In order to retain the snow's brilliance, you give the film more exposure than the meter calls for—one or two stops is usually satisfactory. With an unusually dark subject, the procedure is reversed.

Correct interpretation of a meter reading requires that you know the metering pattern in use. The meter may be taking an average reading of the entire scene, reading a central spot, or giving weight to a central area. Older cameras use one of these methods, while newer, auto-exposure models offer a selection of up to five metering patterns.

PRACTICAL EXPOSURE TIPS

The f/16 rule. Proper exposure results if you set the shutter speed at the reciprocal of the film speed (1/100 second for ISO 100 film) and the aperture at f/16. Vary the exposure by one stop if it is lightly overcast (visible shadows), two stops for heavy overcast (no shadows) and three stops if the subject is in the shade on a sunny day. Because f/stops and shutter speeds are reciprocal, you can easily

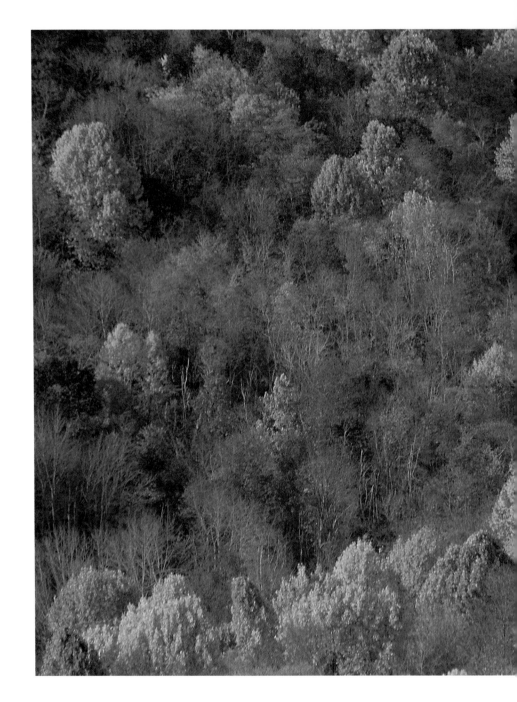

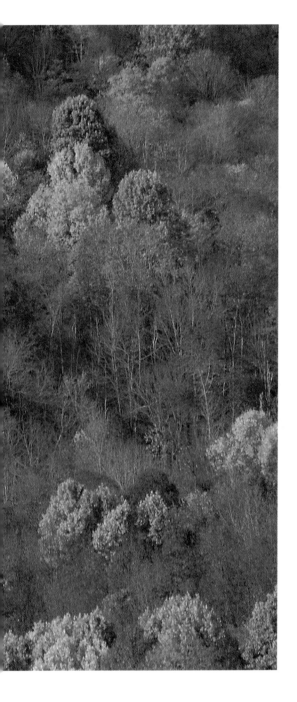

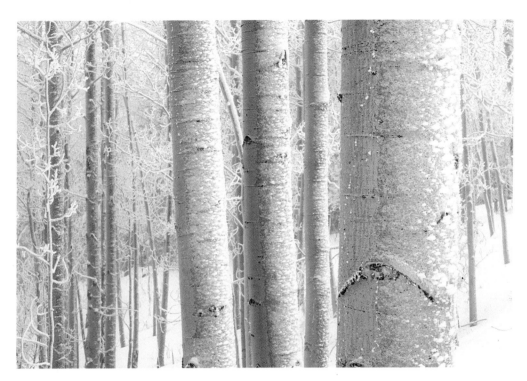

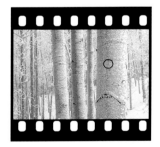

Icy Aspens, San Juan Mountains, Colorado. *The unusual brightness of this scene made it necessary to base the exposure on a spot-meter reading of the bark (see film clip). An average reading of the scene would have darkened the snow and robbed the scene of its drama.*

Adirondack Mountainside, New York. *Due to the even distribution of color and uniform brightness in this scene, an average reading of the entire field resulted in satisfactory exposure. Unlike the accompanying photograph, this picture would be accurately recorded by auto-exposure methods.*

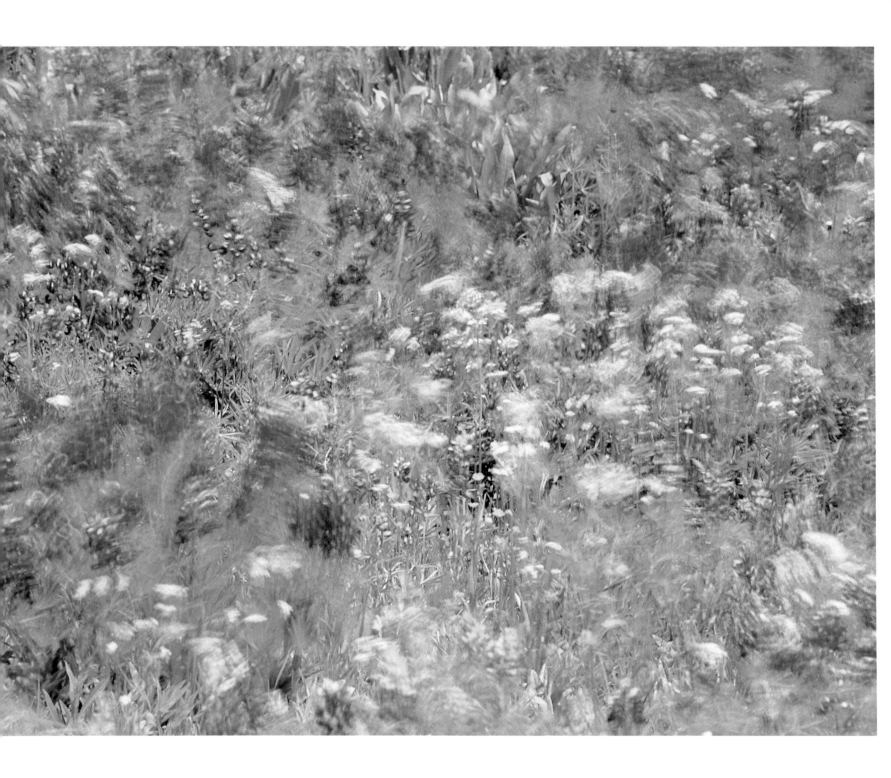

extrapolate any combination desired from these basic settings.

The gray card. Sold in camera stores, the standard gray card reflects 18% of the light that hits it, the same as the average subject for which your light meter is programmed. Held close in front of the lens under the same light that is hitting the scene, it assists in determining exposure in high contrast situations. If you don't have a gray card, take a close-up reading of the palm of your hand, and open up one stop.

Look for a mid-tone. Take a spot-meter reading of an area of the picture that is of average brilliance and use these settings as the basis for the exposure. If your camera doesn't have a spot meter, move closer or temporarily mount a telephoto lens so that the viewfinder is filled by the mid-tone area. If the scene

Giant Sequoia Grove, Yosemite, California. *In overcast conditions such as this, where there are no cast shadows, the f/16 rule (see previous page) is a reliable means of checking exposure settings. Here, soft lighting permits fine detail to be recorded in all parts of the scene.*

Mountain Meadow, Crested Butte, Colorado. *This picture was made by double exposure. Each exposure was made with 1/2 the light needed for correct exposure; that is each was underexposed by one stop. I made the first exposure with a brief shutter speed and precise focus on selected flowers. The second was made with a shutter speed of 1 second to allow the windblown flowers to blur.*

📷 YOSEMITE NATIONAL PARK *SCENIC HOTSPOT*

YOSEMITE IS known for its waterfalls streaming over granite cliffs 2,000 feet high. However, there are other attractions in this 1,200 square miles of wilderness. Yosemite Valley forms the park's nucleus. It is a seven mile corridor crowded with some of the most breath-taking scenery in the world—fast flowing streams, shining lakes, and immense rock formations with names which bespeak their grandeur—Half Dome, El Capitan, Clouds Rest. The alpine habitat, which dominates the park, is strewn with wildflower meadows and glaciated peaks over 13,000 feet. Between elevations of 4,500 and 7,500 feet are groves of giant sequoias with reddish, buttressed trunks 20-30 feet in diameter and heights exceeding 250 feet.

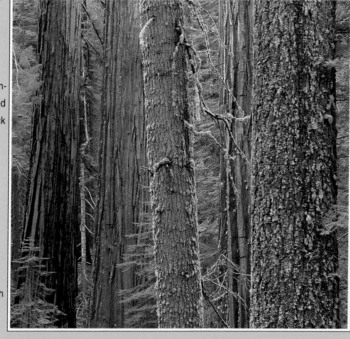

Yosemite is worth visiting any time of the year. In spring, the waterfalls are fullest. They dwindle to a trickle by summer when warm weather brings out the wildflowers and, unfortunately, thousands of tourists. Winter is my favorite time. Crowds are at a minimum, the mountains and valleys are dressed in snow, the light is soft and low for most of the day, and frequent storms bring shifting effects to the landscape. If you are flying, San Francisco is the closest big city, but it's still a five hour drive to the park boundary. The eastern approach by road from Lee Vining is closed by heavy snow except from mid-May to late October. Accommodations are plentiful in the area, with motels, hotels, and national park lodges, cabins, and campsites. Reservations are necessary during the summer. For information, write Yosemite National Park, P.O. Box 577, Yosemite National Park, California 95389.

Snowmass Mountain at Maroon Lake, Colorado. *Frontlighting is appropriate for showing color. It subdues texture and depth. This most photographed scene in the Rockies is best captured at sunrise when the lake is calm and tourists are unlikely to intrude on the view.*

Shiprock, New Mexico. *The dry, clear atmosphere of the American Southwest does little to diffuse the light. About an hour after sunrise, contrast levels are too high to be accurately recorded by most slide films. The key to consistent, high quality photos is to restrict shooting to sunrise and sunset. In this photo the first weak rays of the rising sun bathe the monolith in soft light. Sidelighting reveals the rock's dramatic textures and form.*

Raven and Saguaros, Arizona. *Backlighting is often used most effectively when the subject is translucent (the spines of the cacti) and can be photographed against a dark background (a shaded hillside). I took this photo in the late afternoon, making sure that the lens was well shaded to prevent light from directly striking the front elements.*

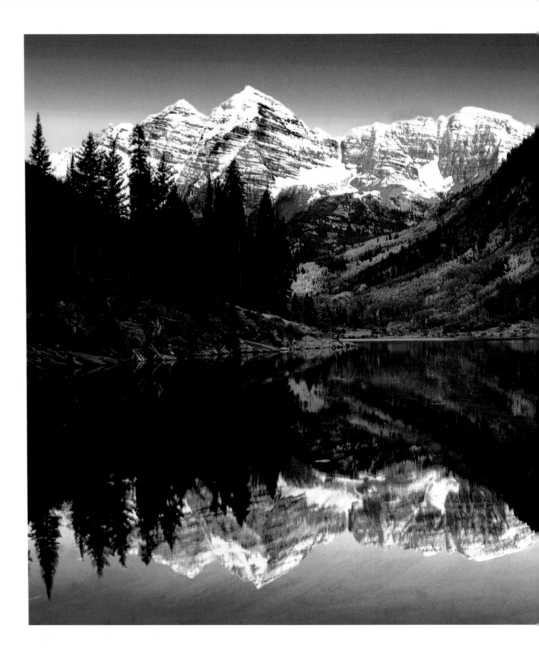

has no mid-tone, meter something nearby that does. Just make sure it is in the same light as the intended composition.

Bracket important shots. When exposure is tricky, you can take some extra insurance pictures at different exposures. Usually it is sufficient to vary the exposure by one stop over and one stop under at one half stop intervals—four extra shots.

LIGHT DIRECTION AND CREATIVITY

Evaluating light intensity and understanding its relationship to consistent, accurate exposure is the basis of photography. The light's direction, or the angle at which it strikes the scene, is the most crucial element in creative photography. The most attractive light occurs when the sun is low in the sky. At this time, you can choose the direction at which light strikes the landscape by changing the camera angle.

Backlighting is commonly chosen for its ability to cast a halo of warm light about individual elements in the landscape. The effect is most dramatic on a subject which is translucent. The limbs of a bare, winter tree, for example, block the light, and appear in silhouette when backlit. During autumn its leaves will glow magically under the same conditions. In such situations, exposure determination is difficult and bracketing is recommended. Silhouetting works best when the sky is rich in color, something which happens for a few minutes before and after sunrise and sunset. It is most effective to place the silhouetted elements of the

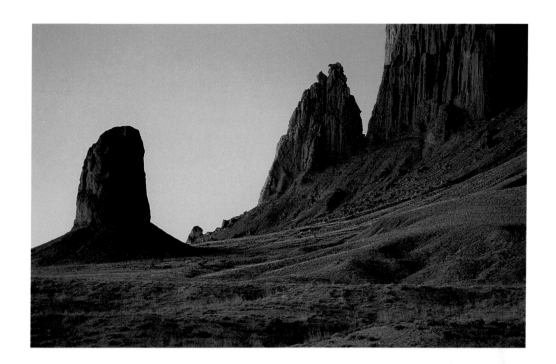

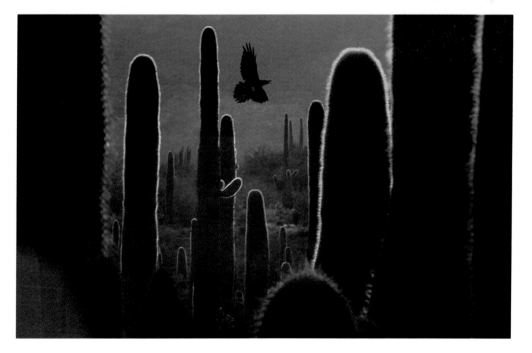

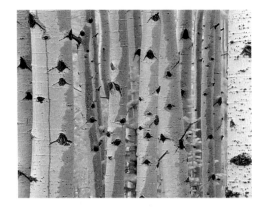

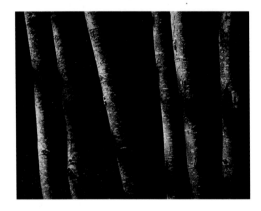

Aspen Grove, Colorado. *Although undramatic, the lighting on overcast days is ideal for showing rich, detailed color. The even illumination brings all areas of a scene within the exposure latitude of most films. In this photo, perspective was compressed and precise framing achieved with an 80 mm—200 mm zoom lens set at minimum aperture (f/22) for maximum depth-of-field.*

Red Alder Grove, Washington. *Sunlight on clear days is high in contrast, creating dark shadows and very bright highlights. In this photo, I exposed for the highlights which produced underexposed shadow areas without detail.*

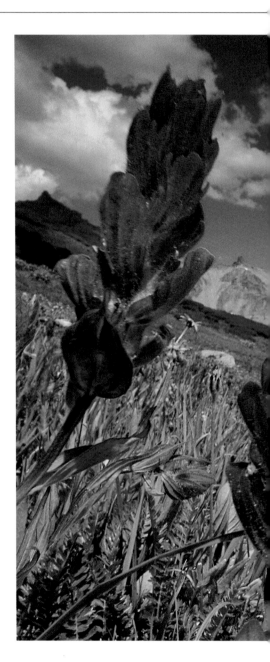

scene on an uncluttered horizon, achieved by keeping the camera low to the ground or selecting a low elevation shooting site.

Frontlighting is appropriate for showing rich color. It produces the most intense and even illumination, de-emphasizing perspective and texture.

Sidelighting casts the longest shadows over the surface of the land, revealing wrinkles, dimples, ridges, and other details of texture in greatest relief. Sidelighting magically transforms the flat surface of a photograph into an image that is strongly three dimensional.

LIGHT TEXTURE AND CONTRAST

Dealing with image contrast is crucial to producing professional quality photographs. Ideally, the contrast, or range of brightness, of the scene will fall within the film's exposure latitude. Low contrast lighting occurs on overcast days, when clouds break up the light, scattering the sun's rays and eliminating distinct shadows. This is called soft light and it is ideal for expressing color, but not so good for showing the contour of the land.

Clear days produce hard light which results in contrast that usually exceeds the exposure latitude of the film. Consequently, the photographer must decide which parts of the scene are to receive proper exposure. If priority is given to the brightest areas (highlights), as is usually preferable, the dark areas (shadows) will be underexposed and lose detail. The reverse will be true if you give priority to the shadows. Excessive con-

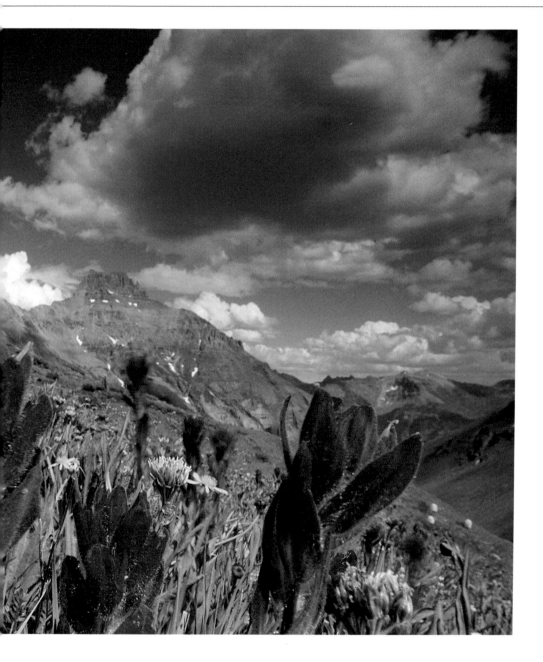

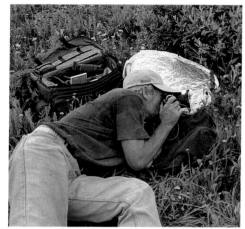

Yankee Boy Basin, Colorado. *Because of the high contrast light on this sunny day, I used a portable reflector to throw light into the shadow areas of the Indian paintbrushes in the photo's foreground. The extreme perspective is produced by a 20 mm lens positioned at ground level only inches from the wildflowers. I adjusted the view so that the flowers framed the mountains in the distance. Exposure was set at 1/15 second and f/16 for maximum depth-of-field.*

📷 **PRINCE EDWARD ISLAND** *SCENIC HOTSPOT*

THIS PARK encompasses a strip of shoreline stretching along the northern coast of Prince Edward Island for 25 miles. It is a fragile seascape of red sandstone cliffs and headlands, and shifting sand dunes spilling out onto sweeping beaches. Behind the dunes are saltwater marshes, shallow ponds and streams. Upland areas are covered with forests of birch, fir, and spruce. It's the only spot I know in North America where red rock formations can be photographed in juxtaposition with blue seas. In addition to exploring these color relationships, you can direct your attention to the expected imagery of the seaside—waves, fog and mist, sunsets and sunrises, dune patterns, and cloud formations. The east/west orientation of the park results in attractive sidelighting at both sunrise and sunset. Because vegetation has little importance as subject matter, there is no prime shooting season. The winter months bring snow and ice to the shoreline which makes the color of the rocks seem even more exotic. During July and August, the weather is the most pleasant, but the beaches are crowded. Prince Edward Island National Park is reached by ferry from Cape Tormentine in New Brunswick and Pictou in Nova Scotia. There are several campsites within the park, and abundant motels, hotels, and bed-and-breakfast lodging only minutes from the beaches. For information contact Prince Edward Island National Park, 2 Palmers Lane, Charlottetown, P.E.I., Canada C1A 5V6

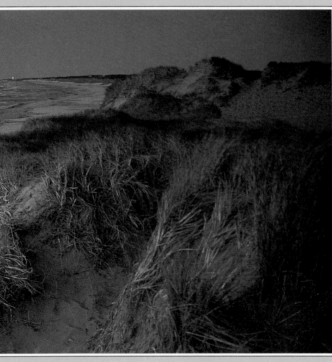

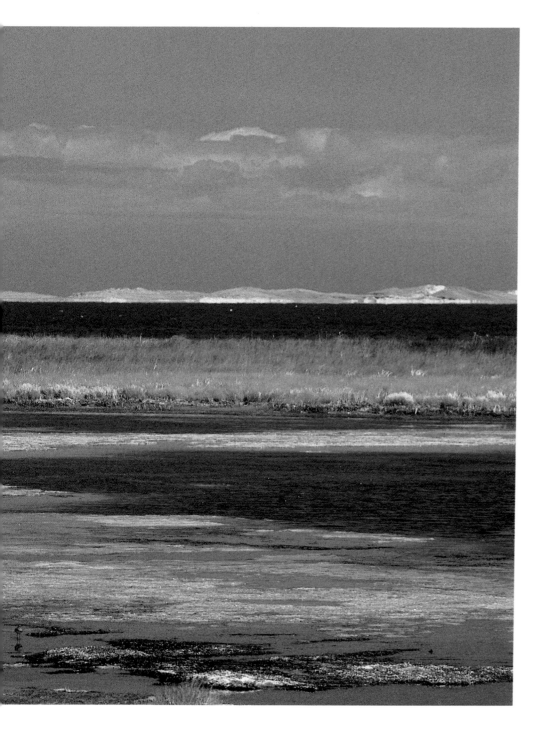

trast is extreme at midday, a time when most photographers advisedly refrain from shooting. Although encountered less frequently, scenes with inherent high contrast, such as black rocks on a white sand beach, can also exceed the film's latitude, regardless of the lighting conditions.

LIGHT COLOR AND MOOD

Light reflected from a blue sky has a blue cast which can be readily seen in the shadows of a photographed snow scene. The light at sunset or sunrise has a warm cast due to the filtering effects of dust and other particles suspended in the air. To the naked eye, the color cast usually goes unnoticed, but not to the camera. Light's inherent color has a significant impact on the overall feeling, or mood, of the image. You can accept the natural color bias that nature imparts to the scene, or use color-correcting filters to remove it.

Sand Dunes, Prince Edward Island. *Taken a few minutes after sunset, this scene is softly illuminated by light reflected from the sky and clouds overhead. A variable neutral density filter was used to darken the sky in the photo's background.*

Marshes, Prince Edward Island. *Although taken during midday when lighting contrast is greatest, this photo shows good detail throughout due to the flat shadowless terrain. I used a 200 mm telephoto lens set at minimum aperture for maximum depth-of-field.*

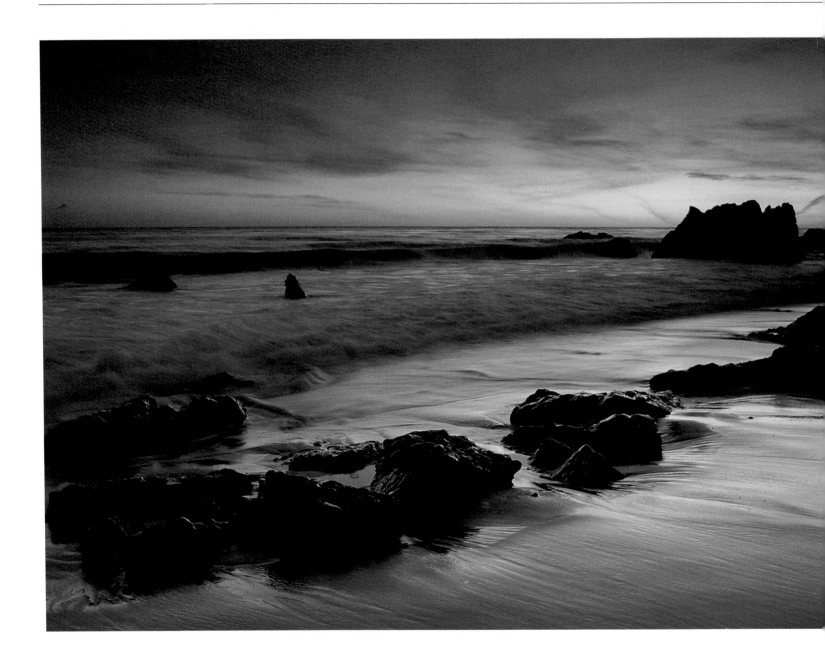

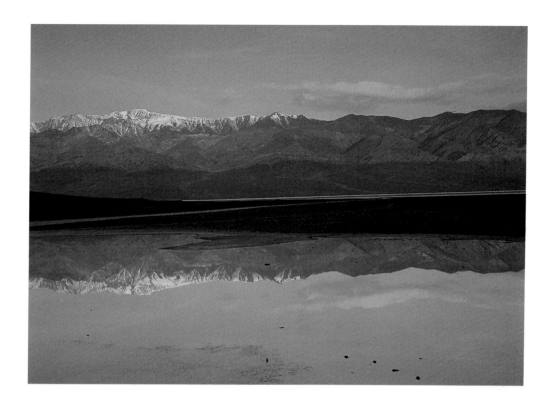

THE BEST TIME TO SHOOT

Except when it is overcast, you should restrict photography to three periods of the day. These periods are all characterized by soft-textured light that reduces contrast problems.

The first priority when composing a picture is the angle of illumination. For example, a mountain range running north/south is frontlit at sunrise and backlit at sundown, two very different visual effects. On the other hand, an east/west range will either be lit from the left or right, depending on the time of day, a factor usually of little photographic consequence.

Sunset. When the sun is near the horizon, its rays travel further through the atmosphere than when the sun is directly overhead. Even under clear conditions, light is diffused by suspended dust and water vapor. At sunset, the light is softer and more colorful than at sunrise due to the buildup of industrial pollutants and particles stirred by the wind and vehicular traffic.

Sunrise. The light of early morning is similar in quality to that of sunset. Although it is often not as colorful, it has other advantages. The calm atmosphere at dawn offers good conditions for photographing mirrorlike reflections in lakes and pools, or making long exposures of wildflower meadows or forests free of the wind's disturbance.

Evening Twilight. At twilight, the land is illuminated by sunlight reflected from the sky or clouds. The light is not only as soft as on an overcast day, but it is often as colorful as that at sun-

Sunrise at Badwater, Death Valley, California. *Even though the sun has not risen high enough to fully illuminate the mountains, its light is nevertheless as cool as that of midday, a result of the unusual dryness and clear atmosphere in Death Valley. A few minutes after this photo was made, a breeze developed and the magic of the reflection disappeared.*

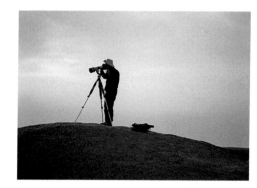

Sunset, Leo Carillo Beach, California. *While waiting for the beautiful light of sunset, I kept busy dodging incoming waves, making sure they did not wash out the sand supporting the tripod. I composed the shot using the rocks as anchor points, and exposed the film for 4 seconds which produced the blurred pattern of the water.*

rise or sunset. Visually there is little difference between morning and evening twilight. But it is much easier to work at the end of the day when you are able to get organized and into position while there is still light. In addition, there are likely to be more clouds to reflect light into the scene.

CLOUDY DAYS

On overcast days, scenic photography loses much of its dramatic potential. The flat, even lighting does not show the form and texture of the land as distinctly as on a clear day. Unless it is stormy, the sky itself has little visual appeal and usually should be excluded from the composition. However, such light is preferred when the color of the subject is more important than form or perspective, as is frequently the case with wildflower meadows and autumn forests. On overcast days, it is best to shoot during the brightest part of the day to maximize the choice of exposure settings.

USING FILTERS

In scenic photography, filters are used primarily to control contrast and enhance color. There are many different brands of screw-in filters. Most are similar in quality so it doesn't pay to spend more money on prestige brands. Cokin makes an extensive system of adjustable filters which are square and fit into holders that screw onto the lens. They are available in two sizes, 'P' (professional/large) and 'A' (amateur/small). The

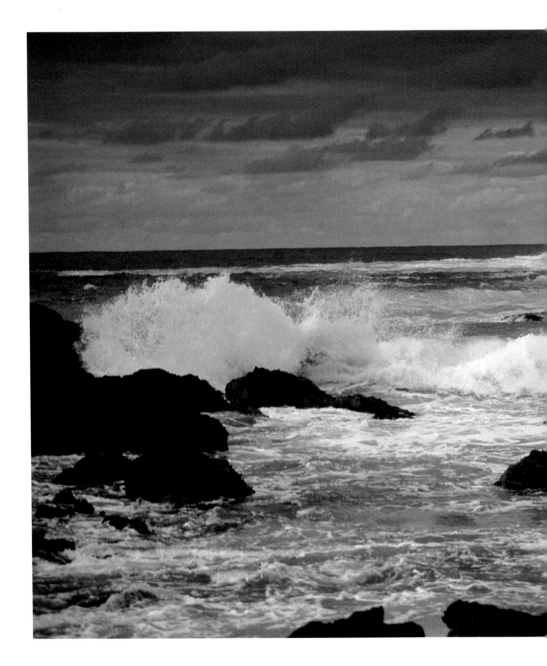

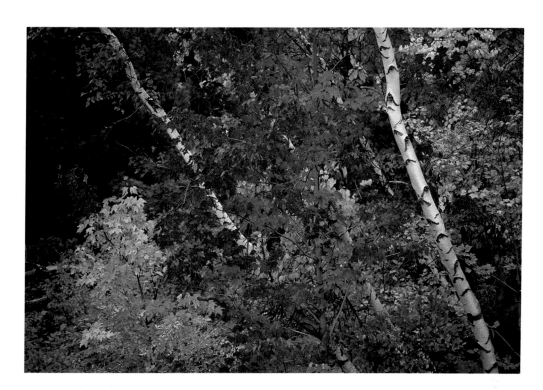

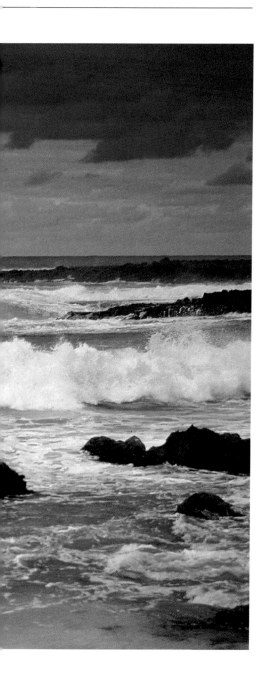

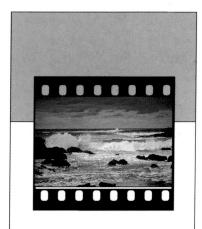

Waimea Bay, Oahu, Hawaii. *The stormy sky of this overcast day was made more dramatic by darkening it with a variable neutral density filter.*

Birch and Maple Grove, New York. *The colors in this photo appear saturated because of the soft, overcast light and the use of two filters—a polarizing filter, which reduced reflections from the foliage, and a warming filter (1a), which imparted a slight orange-red color cast to the image.*

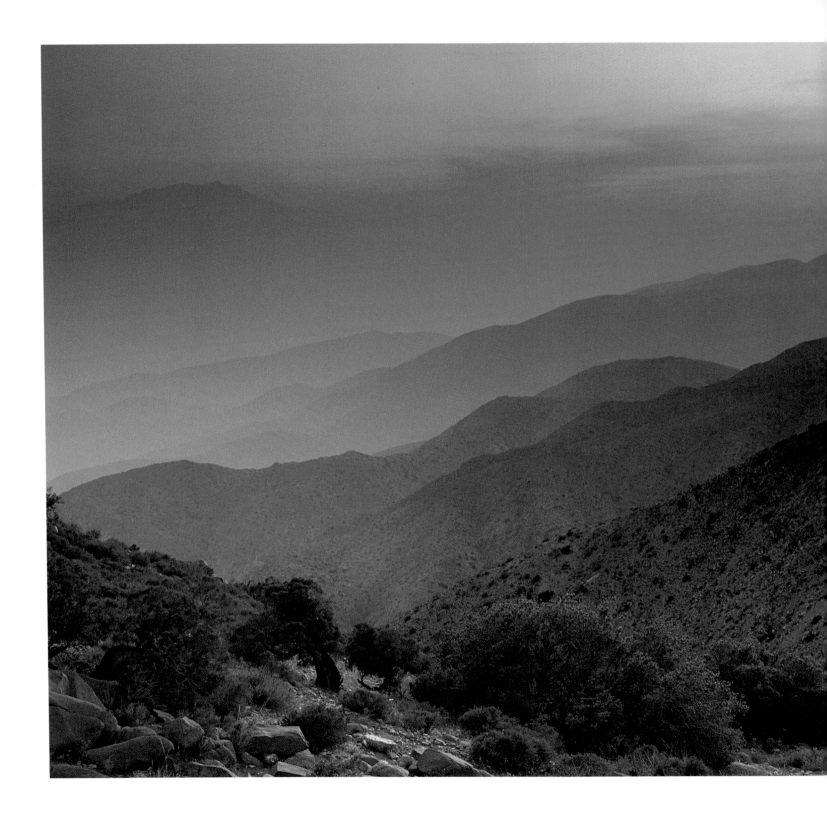

small size is inadequate for large element, wide-angle lenses. Cokin filters are high in quality, relatively inexpensive, and unrivalled in utility and ease of use. No scenic photographer should be without them.

Contrast Control Filters. The best scenic photographers are experts at evaluating and controlling image contrast, most of which emanates from the light source. Restricting shooting to certain periods of the day does much to reduce contrast problems. Contrast can be controlled further with the use of graduated neutral density filters. Those made by Cokin are the best designed and easiest to use. The rectangular filter is half clear and half neutral density (gray). It is mounted on the lens in a holder that allows the filter to be rotated at any angle and adjusted laterally over the scene. Contrast is reduced by positioning the gray portion of the filter over the brightest area of the scene, usually the sky. In some situations, the filter can be positioned to correct excessive contrast within landforms, such as when one side of a of mountain or canyon lies in bright sun and the other is in shade. The filtered result shows much better shadow detail, and even with a two stop filter, retains the look of a sunlit landscape.

Polarizing Filters. I keep polarizing filters attached to my lenses all the time. They produce greater color saturation by reducing or eliminating reflected glare from non-metallic surfaces like leaves, grass, and water. They also darken blue skies dramatically when photographed at right

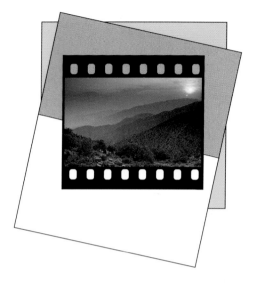

San Jacinto Mountains, Joshua Tree National Monument, California. *Whenever the sun is included in the composition, contrast increases beyond the exposure latitude of any film. I used two variable neutral density filters to decrease the brilliance of the upper portion of the picture, angling them to match the slope of the foreground plane. In addition, I added a warming filter to accentuate the orange tones of the sunset.*

49

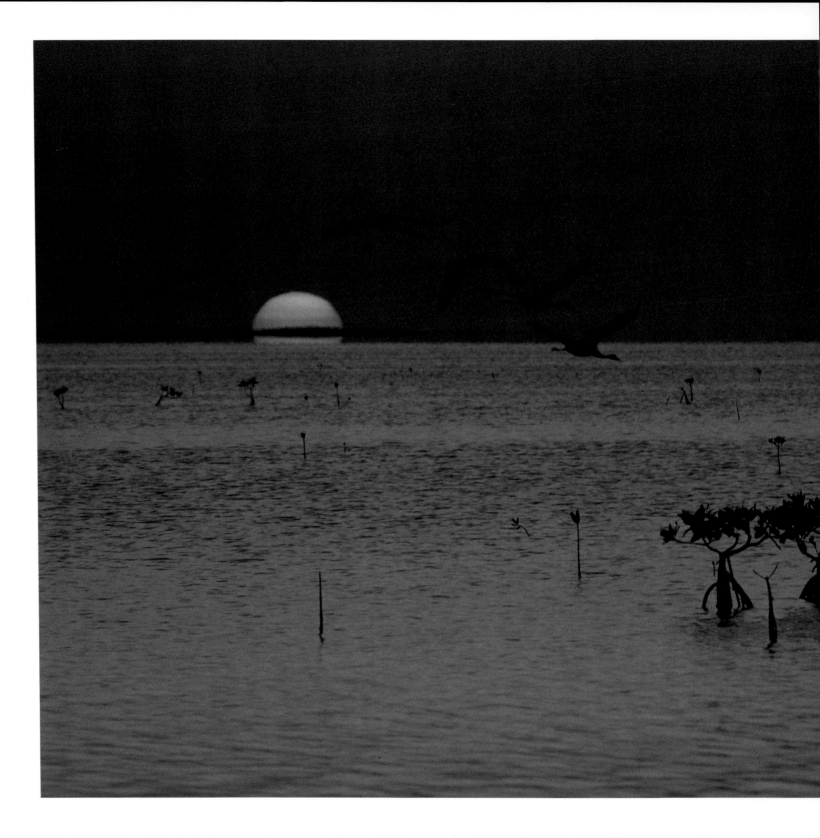

angle to the sun. These filters reduce scene brightness by one to two stops. They are thick and may cut off part of the view, especially with wide-angle lenses. Before buying one, attach the filter to your lens and view a bright light source with the lens stopped down to minimum aperture. Check the corners of the viewfinder to see if the frame has been cut off. Also, make certain to check your camera manual to find out whether a regular, or circular, polarizer is required.

Graduated Color Filters. Made by Cokin in a variety of colors, these adjustable, rectangular filters are half clear and half color. They are used in the same way as the graduated neutral density filters, except the colored portion is positioned in front of an area you wish to emphasize. For example, a blue filter can be used to intensify a blue sky without affecting exposure or color hue as happens with polarizing filters. Cokin filters are made in two different densities in a large variety of colors. I carry blue, yellow, green, and pink.

Color Enhancing Filter. This filter is used to accentuate oranges and reds. It causes unexpected color shifts and requires an exposure increase of about one to two stops. Its effect is most pleasing with fall colors and blue skies, although the skies take on a violet hue. It is expensive, so you might wish to buy one to fit your largest diameter lens and use step-down rings to attach it to smaller lenses.

Warming Filters. Not to be confused with color enhancing filters, this amber filter imparts a yellow-orange hue throughout the scene. Most photo-

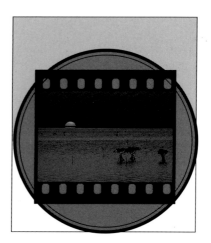

Sandhill Cranes, Florida Coast. *This image is a composite made of two slides taken at different times and places. The scenic photo was shot at f/8 and 8 seconds using a polarizing filter to remove reflections from the water and a graduated neutral density filter to darken the sun and sky so they fell within the exposure latitude of the film. The cranes were shot with a 500 mm lens at 1/250 second against an overcast sky at Bosque del Apache National Wildlife Refuge in New Mexico.*

51

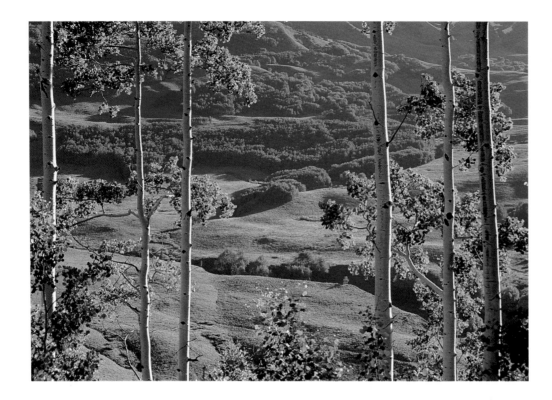

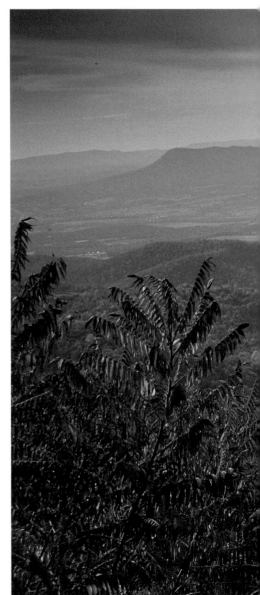

graphers use an 81A (least effect) or 81B (moderate effect) to warm up the scene without creating a color shift.

FILM

If light is the brush that creates the photograph, film is the paint it is dipped in. Modern photographic film is made up of an emulsion of light sensitive chemicals laminated to plastic acetate. Scenic 35 mm photography is nearly always done with color film. To most people, color imagery is more appealing, and to the photographer, it is a much richer medium for creative expression. Black and white scenic photography is carried out with larger format cameras using sheet film which enables the photographer to custom develop individual negatives to achieve a greater control over image contrast.

A film's sensitivity is rated in ISO numbers (printed on the film cassette). The smaller the number, the lower the sensitivity of the film. Slow films (ISO 50 and lower) provide the most detail and the richest color. They produce the highest quality images and are therefore preferred for landscape photography. Fast films (ISO 200 and higher) react quickly to light and allow the photographer to use brief shutter speeds. These films are suitable for handheld camera work, sports, and wildlife. Medium speed films are a compromise between speed and image quality.

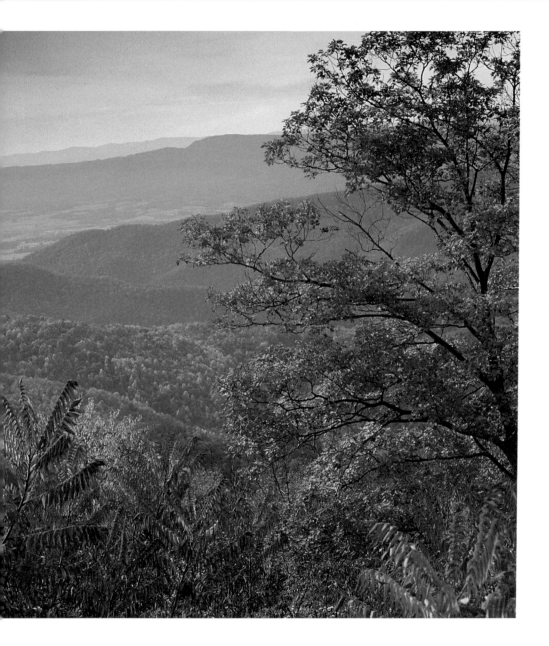

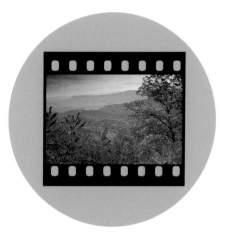

Shenandoah National Park, Virginia. I used a color enhancing filter to accentuate the color of the autumn foliage in this photo. In contrast to the more standard warming filters, color enhancing filters produce greater saturation in only the warmer portion of the spectrum.

Aspens, San Juan Mountains, Colorado. In this photo, both UV (ultraviolet) and polarizing filters were used to reduce haze and foliage reflections, resulting in more saturated color.

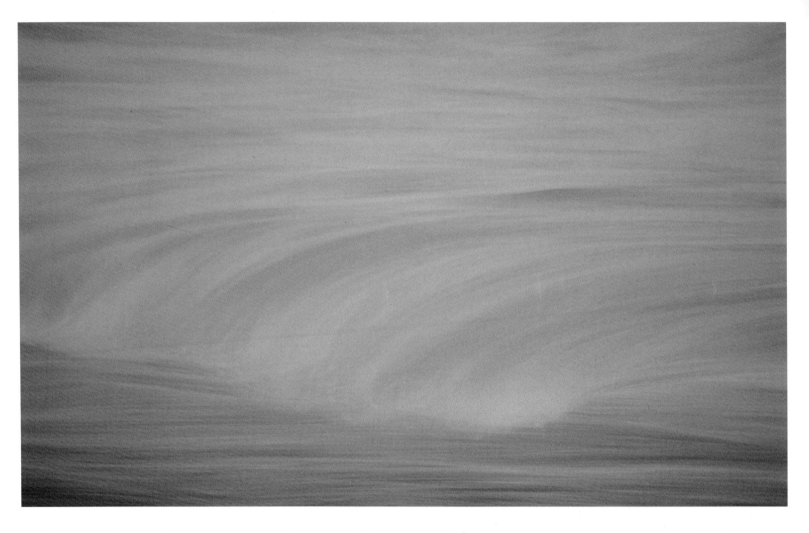

Transparency film is used by most landscape photographers. It produces images with more detail and richer color than negative film. Transparencies can be viewed directly by means of a magnifier (loupe), projected onto a screen, or made into high quality prints. Transparencies produce the best color reproduction for calendars, magazines, and books. The following list describes the transparency films popular with professional photographers and picture editors.

Kodachrome 25. Once the standard by which other color films were measured, Kodachrome 25 provides fine detail and accurate, natural color.

Ektachrome Elite 50. Although twice as fast as Kodachrome 25, this relatively new film is unexcelled in rendering fine detail. It is designed to enhance the color of a scene.

Ektachrome Elite 100. With detail and color nearly equal to its big brother, this is a great all-around film. Its extra speed is useful to arrest subject motion such as windblown foliage.

Fujichrome Velvia 50. This film is comparable to Ektachrome Elite 50 in rendering detail and enhancing color.

Ektachrome Lumiere. This is a professional version of Elite 100, with more consistent color balance and light sensitivity. These are minor advantages which are more than offset by Lumiere's need for refrigeration and a price nearly double that of comparable films.

📷 WATERFALLS AND RUSHING RIVERS *SPECIAL SITUATION*

SURF BREAKING on a rocky beach, the plunge of a river over a cliff, or the gentle trickling of a summer stream all provide opportunity to explore motion. Choosing a shutter speed that produces blur in a waterfall or river enhances the sensuous movement of the water. The blurring should be obvious to eliminate any confusion about the photographer's intention. The shutter speed depends on the speed of the water, but in most cases an exposure of 1/15 second, or longer, is needed. You should use a tripod, and if possible, include stationary elements in the composition to accentuate by contrast the water's movement. Water courses with froth or bubbles yield the most pleasing

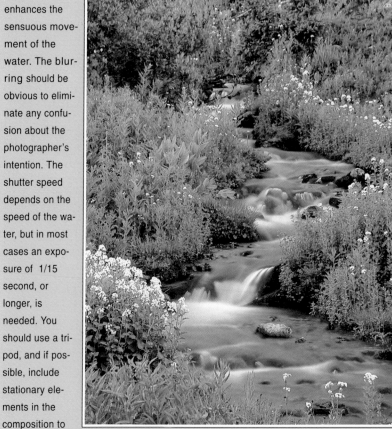

results because the stream of bubbles fuses into a white swirl on film.

When photographing the ocean, especially breaking surf, each wave exhibits a unique configuration. They are apt subjects for stop-action photography. Interesting pictures also result by panning along with a wave as it moves toward shore at a slow shutter speed—1/15 or 1/30 second. As you follow the wave, try to pan across stationary elements such as rocks or trees which will introduce streaking patterns into the composition and enhance the feeling of motion.

Rushing Waves, Hawaii. *Using a slow shutter speed is one of the most effective ways to express motion. In this photo, I used a handheld camera with 200 mm lens, set at f/16 and 1/15 second, and panned along with the wave as it moved past me. To photograph waves at such an angle while on shore, you must position yourself on a spit or pier that extends out into an area of water where wave action is strong.*

Alpine Stream, Colorado. *Showing the blurred motion of water can be dramatized by including in the composition elements that are sharply rendered. This photo was taken on a still evening just after sunset using a 10 second exposure.*

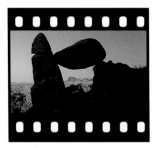

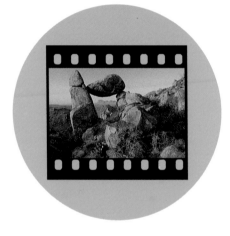

Window Rock, Big Bend National Park, Texas.
My first hike into this location was timed to record the view at sunset. I arrived only to find the rock window in deep shade. The next morning I was set up to shoot about 15 minutes before sunrise. I used a color enhancing filter to accentuate the rocks, but it also imparted a violet hue to the sky. The film used was the same as for most pictures in this book, Fujichrome Velvia, my favorite.

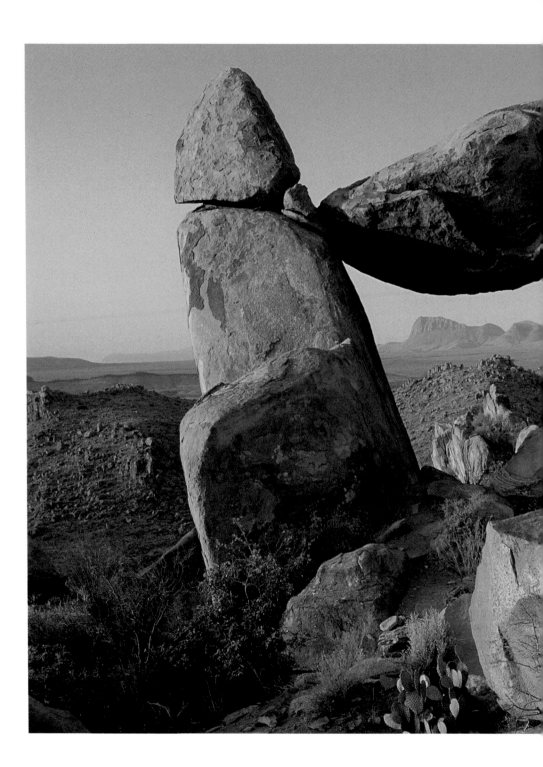

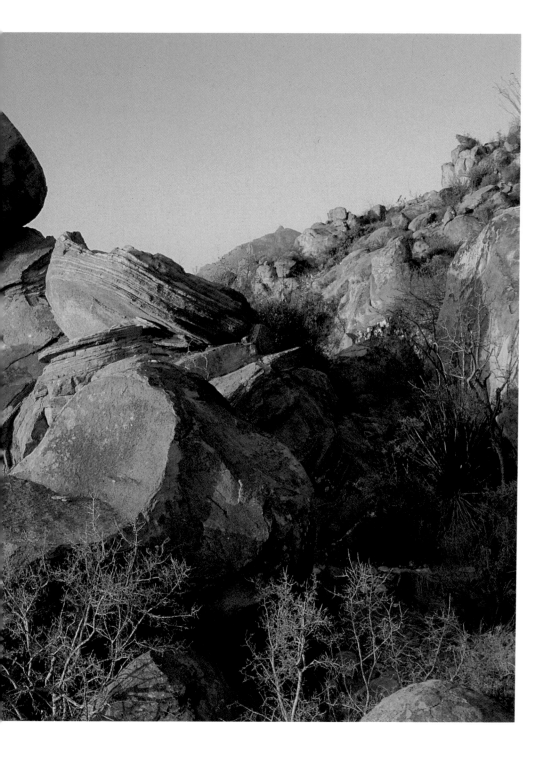

FILM HANDLING

Film should be stored in a cool, dry, dark environment. When at home, I keep my film in the refrigerator. When on the road, I pack it in ziplock freezer bags, with an assortment of ten rolls per bag. I store them in a picnic cooler (no ice). I also carry pre-addressed, stamped processing mailers so that exposed film can be mailed for processing without delay. Kodak PK Processing Mailers provide inexpensive, good quality processing, and quick turnaround (about one week including shipping time).

PART III

Composition

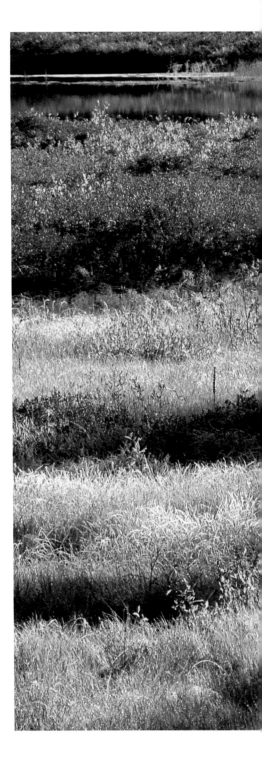

WHEN A SCENIC photographer looks into the viewfinder, he is usually confronted with a jumble of features—lakes, rivers, forests, meadows—whatever happens to be part of the landscape under consideration. These features are made up of graphic elements of line, shape, texture, and color. Composition is the way the photographer chooses to arrange these elements. This process is most productive when the photographer first establishes the photograph's theme—the message that he wishes the picture to convey.

DOMINANCE

Some picture elements attract the eye more than others. For example, red is more exciting than blue, jagged lines are more striking than curved ones, diagonal lines are more attractive than vertical ones, rough textures are more exciting than smooth

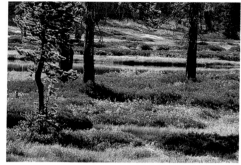

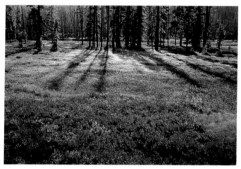

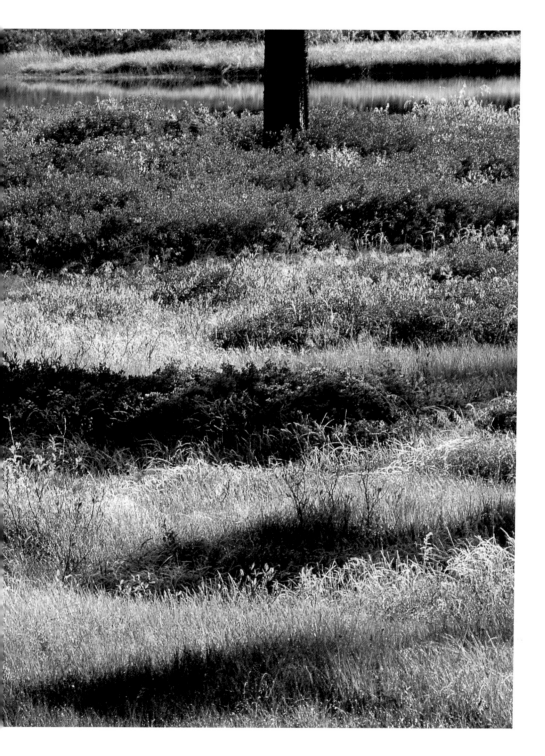

Frosted Meadows, Banff National Park, Alberta.
I was initially attracted to the rich color, frost, and elongated shadows of this scene. Although the first two versions (above) are not without merit, consideration of the many attractive visual elements as I was working out the composition gradually led me to the picture at left. It is preferred for its focus on but a few elements—frost, warm colors, and horizontal shadow pattern. These were easily isolated by changing my camera position and the focal length of the zoom lens.

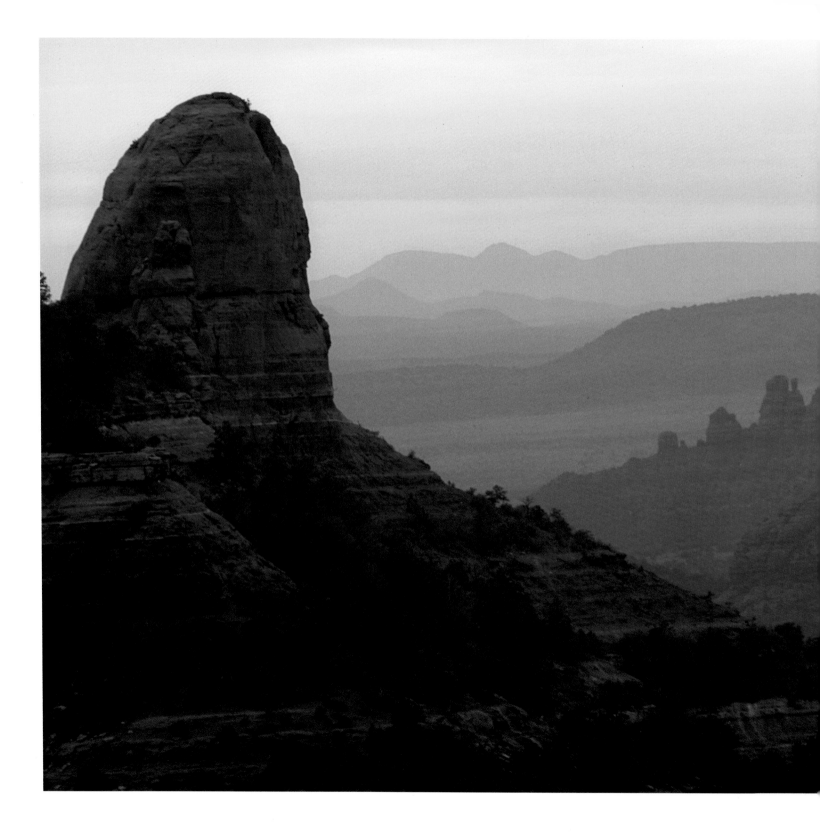

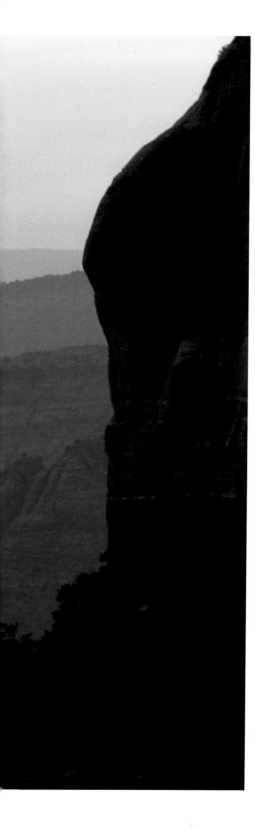

ones. And most important to photography, light is more attractive than dark. I call this the principle of dominance. It works the same whether you intend your pictures for exhibition in Indiana or India.

Few wilderness scenes offer choices as simple as the ones listed above. More often you must compare a curved, brown line with a jagged, yellow one; a gray, diagonal, rough texture with one that is smooth, vertical, and green. Such comparisons sound difficult, but the eye makes the assessments intuitively. The process begins as soon as you look in the viewfinder and begin manipulating picture elements by changing the camera angle, moving closer, or waiting for better light.

At first, you may evaluate what you see in the viewfinder for its emotional, rather than visual, appeal. Suppose you are trying to record the color of a wildflower meadow. You pay no attention to the bright, overcast sky that forms the background. It has little significance until the film is developed—until the multi-sensory experience of the field is transferred onto the flat, silent section of film. Then the colors of the meadow are overwhelmed by the sky's white brilliance.

To avoid such oversights, photographers school themselves to think in graphic terms. The center of interest—the meadow—is perceived as a rectangle of green dabbed with various other colors. For the scene to be effective, the meadow must be more attractive than any other part of the picture. The brilliance of the sky is reduced by

Red Rock Bluffs near Sedona, Arizona. *Usually the theme for a landscape composition is suggested by nature. The photographer's job is to refine and emphasize the design. In this photograph, the receding planes of jagged hills and mountains were dramatically framed by two massive rock outcrops. My task was to isolate this view with the appropriate lens and camera angle, render the entire scene sharply by accurately placing the depth-of-field, and bring the full range of subject brilliance within the esposure latitude of the film (accomplished by the use of an angled, variable neutral density filter). (See below.)*

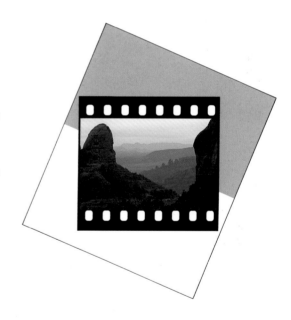

East River near Crested Butte, Colorado.
Taken from a ridge above the river valley, the curved linear elements of this landscape are readily apparent. The first view was taken in early morning when sunlight was reflected from the water's surface. I increased contrast with two angled variable neutral filters, one at top-right, the other at bottom-left, to darken the meadows. Their lack of color and detail emphasizes the shape and sparkle of the river. The second shot, taken from the same position a few hours later, illustrates the variable effects of lighting.

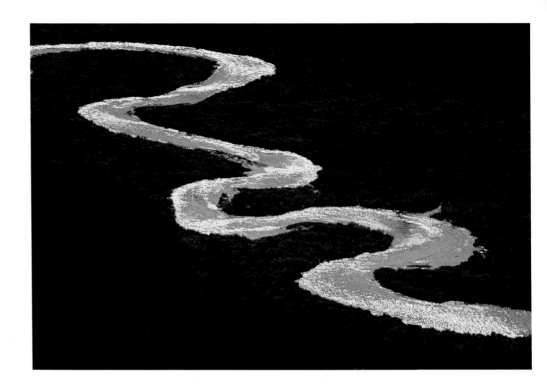

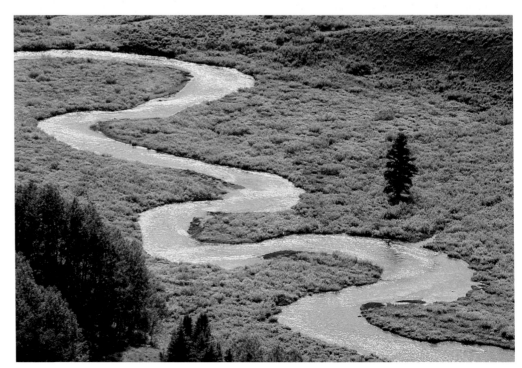

the use of a graduated neutral density filter, or by adjusting the camera angle to eliminate the sky completely.

When shooting, put the drama of the scene out of your mind. A stand of monumental redwoods is perceived as a series of vertical bars, the rising fire of the sun as an orange disc, a pristine mountain lake as an expanse of ripples. View the scene as lines, shapes, textures, and colors. With this approach, the visual strength of each picture element is isolated, facilitating a clearer analysis of the design.

DESIGN ELEMENTS

The world is made up of an infinite changing mix of lines, shapes, textures, and colors. By understanding the graphic essence of these elements, you will be able to manipulate them more effectively when composing photographs.

Shapes are the basic ingredients of most landscape photographs. Mountain peaks and poplar leaves are triangles, tree trunks and rocks are rectangles, hills and setting suns are semi-circles. Most things are variations or combinations of formal geometric shapes. Shapes with sharp corners have the most visual force; smooth shapes have the least.

Lines are not much less than very thin shapes. In a photograph, they set the limits of a space, indicate a direction, or join one part of the scene to another. They do not have much visual substance of their own, but are used to organize

📷 SAN JUAN MOUNTAINS *SCENIC HOTSPOT*

ONE OF NATURE'S unforgettable spectacles is a forest of golden aspen reaching up toward timberline on a high mountain pass in Colorado. Any photographer searching for America's most magnificent landscapes should not miss the San Juan Mountains in late September. However, aspens are not the only attraction. The mountains themselves are the highest in the Rocky Mountain chain. There are numerous passes

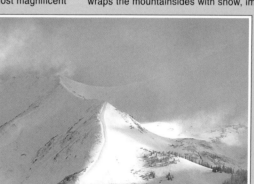

above 9,000 feet accessible by four-wheel drive vehicle (a few by regular passenger car) that allow the photographer to reach stunning alpine panoramas. Shooting is excellent during any season due to the exceptional nature of the topography. During summer, wildflowers are on display in the sub-alpine meadows. At Yankee Boy Basin near Ouray, you will find the most lush and colorful four-wheel drive accessible meadows on the planet. Aspens are the big attraction during the fall and great pictures are possible almost anywhere in the San Juans. Winter wraps the mountainsides with snow, imparting a magical mood and new color scheme to the landscape.

Durango is the most conveniently located town with a commercial airport, although there are many small towns throughout the region. Most were established during the mining boom of the last century. Many have been restored and meet the needs of tourists with accommodations from simple cabins to deluxe resorts, health spas, and ski condos. Four-wheel drive rental vehicles are widely available to get you up to the most scenic locations. For information, write Ouray Visitor Center, P. O. Box 145, Ouray, Colorado 81427.

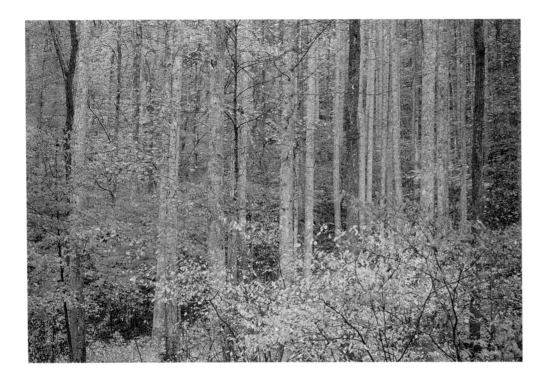

Cove Forest, Great Smoky Mountains National Park, Tennessee. *The texture, so evident in this photograph, is not the result of the lighting, which is soft and without shadow, but rather it is produced by the subtle combination of rich, closely related colors. To achieve the highest quality from lenses and films, avoid using extreme settings, such as minimum or maximum apertures, and exposure times that are longer than one second. This photo was made with a 200 mm lens set at f/11, 1/15 second on Fujichrome Velvia, with a polarizing filter (to remove leaf reflections) and a warming filter (1a).*

Poppy Meadows, Tehachapi Mountains, California. *The repetition of intersecting diagonal lines created by these overlapping hillsides is the basis of this composition. It is easy to overlook such unusual views, especially when confronted with natural scenes as beautiful of these poppy meadows, if you do not make an objective evaluation of the landscape's graphic elements. To exclude any irrelevant visual information that might weaken the pattern, the scene was carefully framed by adjusting the camera angle and magnification of the 80 mm—300 mm zoom lens.*

and support other visual elements. In scenic photography, lines are most often encountered as the borders of intersecting landscape planes and the horizon line.

Although texture appeals to our sense of touch, it is closely related to vision. At a young age, our eyes learn from our fingertips what is pleasant to touch and what is not. By the time we are adults, we do most of our feeling with our eyes. We can see that a sand dune feels like silk, or that a prairie has the texture of brushed mohair. When incorporated into a photograph, the viewer knows that these visual sensations have nothing to do with the actual texture of the landscape, yet they nevertheless heighten the sensory appeal of the image, making it more dynamic and convincing.

COLOR

Color is the most important visual element. Its presence, or absence, is the most significant factor of any design. Color not only projects visual force of its own, but it is an inherent part of every shape, line, and texture which we find in a photograph. Our reaction to color is instinctive. When designing pictures, the manipulation of color is usually concerned with how different colors relate to one another.

The most eye-catching color is red; perhaps because it is the color of blood, a sign of injury, or even death. It is our color of choice for important messages—stop lights, fire exits, and negative

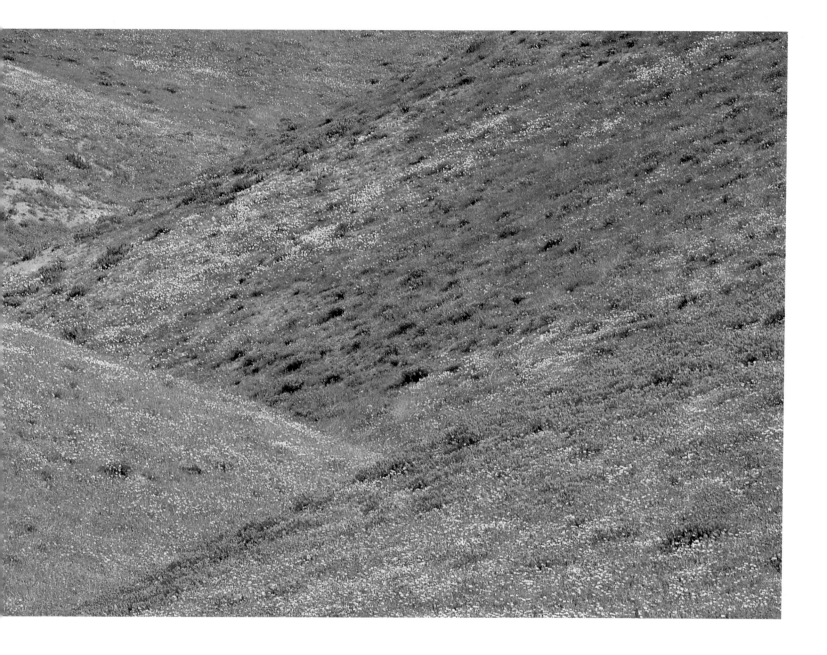

Red Maples and Beeches, Mad River, Vermont.
The juxtaposition of the complimentary red/green hues in this photograph lends intensity to the color. The slow shutter speed (1/8 second), combined with the gentle breeze, produced a secondary contrast between the blurred foliage and the detailed trunks.

Yellow Birch Forest, Adirondack State Park, New York. Intense color is again evident here because of the combination of complimentary hues of yellow and blue. I used an 18 mm lens and a polarizing filter to darken the sky. Even though the exposure was 1/15 second, no tripod was necessary due to the ultra-wide focal length.

Celandine and Black Ash Trees, Turkey Point, Ontario. It is rare to find a patch of wildflowers on the forest floor lush enough to make a strong visual impact in a scenic photograph. Although this photo was made at midday, the light was softened by the forest canopy. I kept the camera angled downward to exclude the sky whose brightness would have dominated the composition.

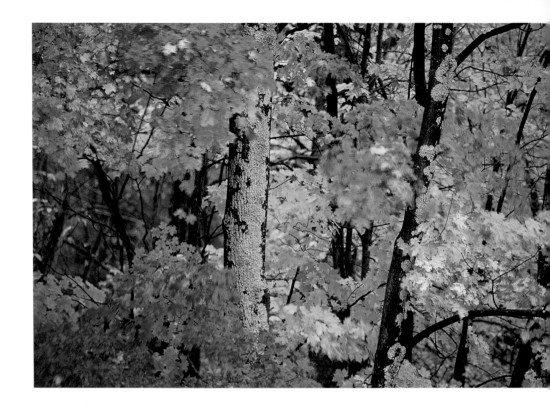

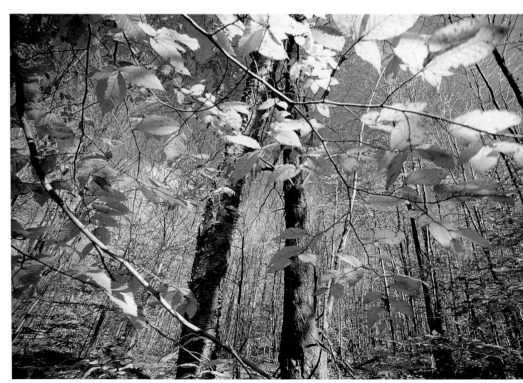

bank balances. Generally, red should be part of the design only if it supports, or is integral to, the center of interest. Warm colors—red, orange, yellow—have more visual strength than cool ones—blues and greens.

A color gains strength when it is juxtaposed with an opposite (complimentary) hue—red with green, orange with blue, yellow with purple. The red of Indian paintbrush, for example, appears more intense when photographed against a blue sky. Intense colors are more attractive than muted ones, but not necessarily more appealing.

The colors in a photograph should support the central theme. A combination of vibrant, contrasting color causes the eye to bounce back and forth between opposing hues and creates visual excitement. It is suited for themes that express action, conflict, joy, anger, celebration, discovery, youth. Contrasting color schemes are volatile and can be confusing. They work best when incorporated into simple designs.

Harmonious color is composed of one or two related hues; blue and turquoise, pink and violet, orange and rust. Such combinations are suited for passive, introspective themes which incorporate smooth shapes and horizontal lines. Compositions based on harmonious color schemes automatically result in a coherent visual effect.

Color tempers all aspects of the design process. It distinguishes the subjects of the composition, communicates mood and emotion, and in many photographs, it acts alone as the central

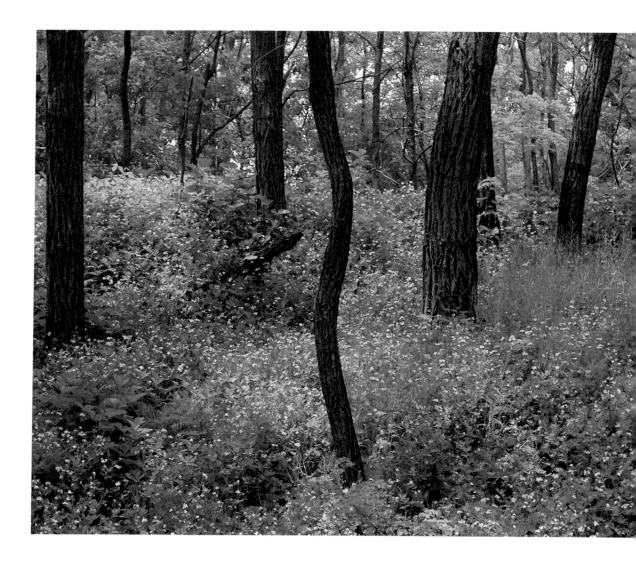

📷 ZION AND BRYCE CANYON *SCENIC HOTSPOT*

ZION AND BRYCE are completely different landscapes, but they are neighboring parks, and few people visit one without taking time to see the other. In Zion National Park, precipitous canyon walls and massive stone monoliths, sculpted over thousands of years by the Virgin River, lie in every direction. The stone formations are on a grand scale, soaring thousands of feet above the lush cottonwoods, oaks, and willows of the canyon floor. Bryce Canyon, little more than an hour's drive to the northeast, is an unrestrained expression in red, orange and pink stone. It is a huge amphitheatre filled with intricate spires, hoodoos, and rock temples sometimes arranged in breathtaking patterns, sometimes thrown together with apparent whimsey. Light reflected through this labyrinth offers fascinating, ever-changing effects.

In both parks, preferred seasons are fall and winter. Autumn brings colorful foliage and dramatic skies. Winter dusts the rocks and trees with white, creating a pure reference against which the eye can measure the landscape's unusual colors. Summer in Zion allows the photographer to capture red rock walls framed by the intense greens of riverside cottonwoods and the laser blue of clear skies. Both parks provide pleasant campgrounds, cabins and lodges within a stone's throw of good places to set-up your tripod. There is an interesting selection of motels and bed-and-breakfast accommodation in Virgin, just outside the western entrance to Zion. The closest, major fly-in destination is Las Vegas, Nevada, less than two hours by car from Zion. For information, write Zion National Park, Springdale, Utah 84767-1099 and Bryce Canyon National Park, Bryce Canyon, Utah 84717.

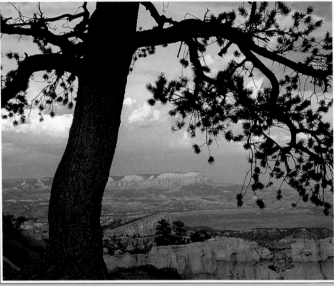

theme. Color is a fundamental part of our perceptive process, our dreams, our memories, our personality. It will most distinguish your photography if you approach it intuitively, and use it in a way which feels right to you.

DESIGN STRATEGY

The photographer uses various strategies to organize the graphic elements in the photograph. No matter which approach you are using, the principle of dominance is fundamental to all design decisions.

CENTER OF INTEREST

Landscape compositions often are organized about a single subject—one peak in a mountain range, a reflection in a lake, a grove of trees, or a waterfall. The center of interest orchestrates the design, determining the nature and arrangement of the other elements of the composition. The process is mainly one of elimination. You frame and focus on the center of interest and then examine the rest of the scene for distracting elements. This includes anything that is brighter, more interesting in shape, or attractive in color. These elements must be eliminated or subdued.

Often, you may incorporate new elements in the scene that reinforce the center of interest—a rock window or overhanging bough that frames the subject; a line, such as a river, or pattern, such as rocks or trees, that leads the eye to the subject.

The position of the main subject within the

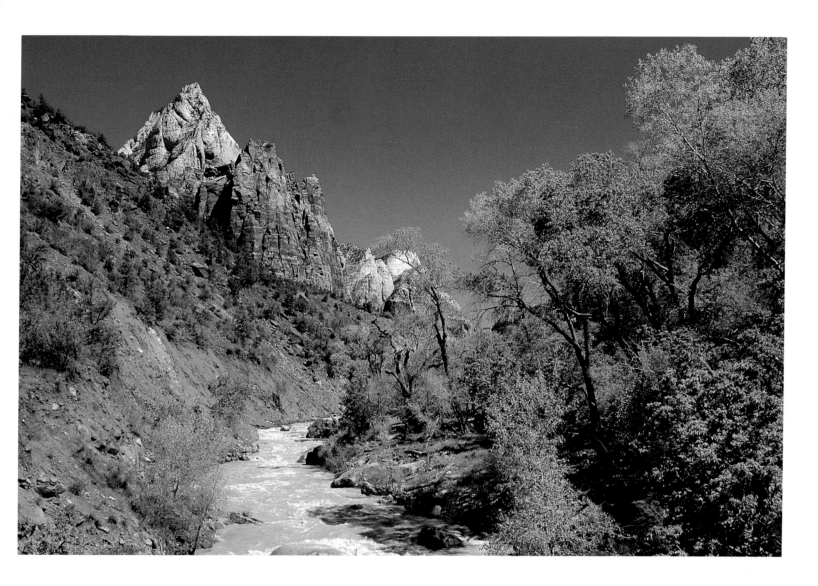

View from Sunset Point, Bryce Canyon National Park, Utah. *The distant rock forms, illuminated by the last rays of the setting sun, are the most attractive elements in this scene, and thus comprise the center of interest of the composition. The foreground tree focuses attention on the center of interest and creates a dramatic impression of depth.*

Virgin River Valley, Zion National Park. *The telescoping shape of the river leads the eye through this composition, giving organization to an otherwise confusing assembly of diverse and powerful picture elements.*

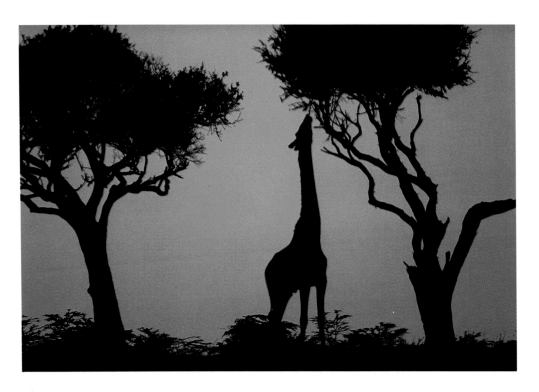

Masai Giraffe, Serengeti Plains, Kenya. *Although there would be little chance of mistaking the center of interest in this picture, the similar graphic quality of the silhouetted giraffe and acacia trees made it advisable to position the animal near the center of the frame. I shot this picture shortly before sunrise with the camera sitting on the ground, propped up with a few pebbles, using a 300 mm lens wide open at 1/125 second.*

Waterton Lakes National Park, Alberta. *With graphic elements very similar in quality to the photo above, this picture is organized differently due to the unique nature of the center of interest. The small, tree-crowned island, projecting above the horizon and backlit by the rising sun, has ample graphic power to be positioned away from the center, giving a dynamic order to the composition.*

frame is dependent on other elements of the composition. The prime real estate of any picture is the center. This is where the eye enters the composition and begins its exploration. If you place the main subject here, the eye locates it quickly, scrutinizes it, then scans the remainder of the frame for anything else of interest. As it has already found the most compelling element, it soon returns for another, likely final, look. The design is static.

But suppose you place the main subject somewhere other than the center. The eye starts in the center, finds nothing of interest, and begins to search the picture field. Eventually, it finds the main subject, but on the way it has come across other interesting elements which you may have included to support the main subject. Now the eye is having fun. When all is seen, it gravitates back to the center of the frame, but again it finds nothing and begins the search anew, this time likely taking a different path to the main subject. The dynamism of this process excites our visual sense and sustains interest in the photo.

The magnetism of the main subject determines how far from the center it can be placed. A main subject that is visually dominant can be placed almost anywhere in the frame and still be readily identified. If there are other equally powerful visual elements, then it can become dominant only by occupying the central area of the frame.

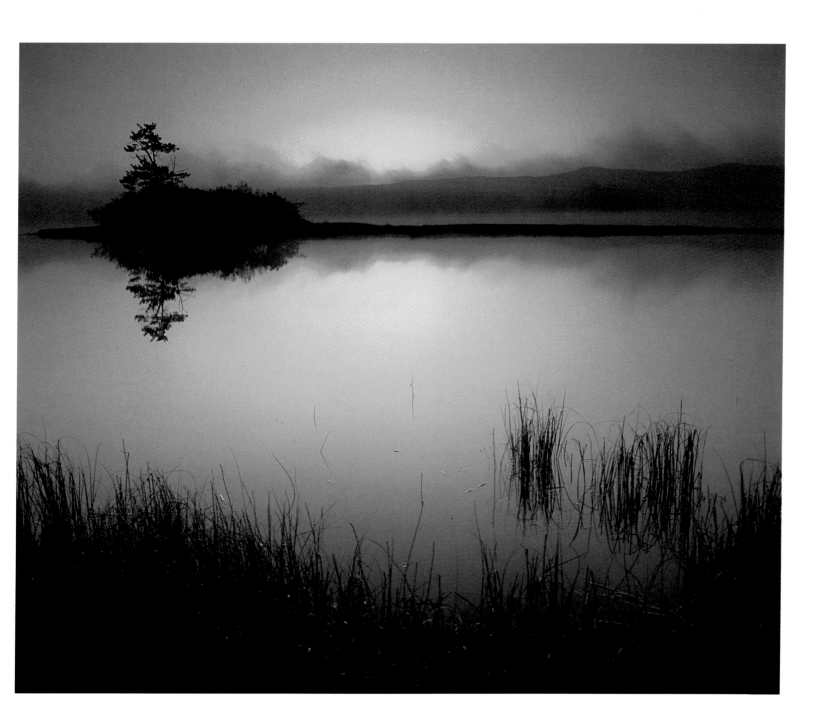

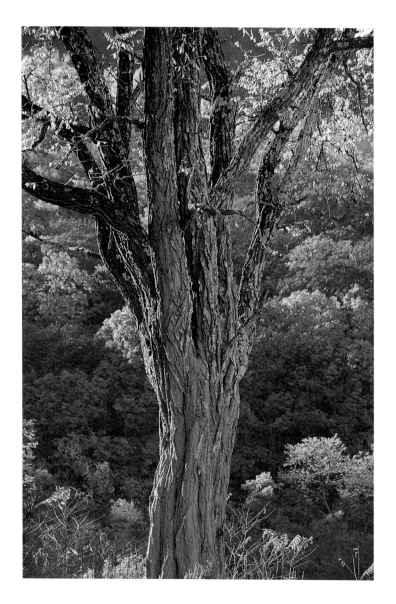

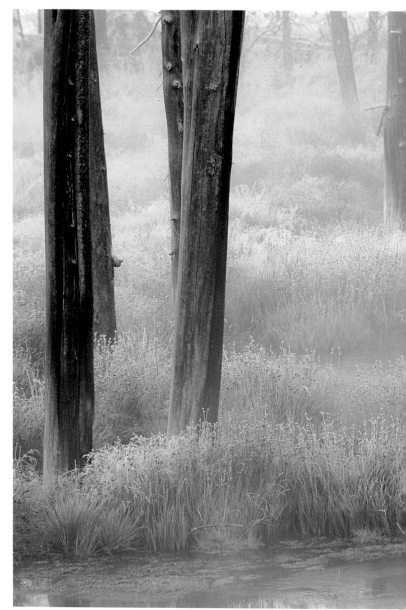

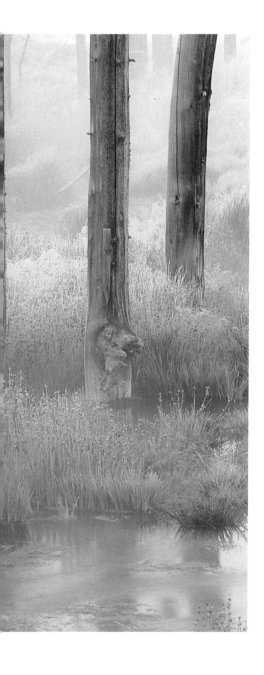

CENTRAL THEME

Compositions may be based on a concept, idea, or relationship, rather than one visual element in the scene. Here, a number of picture elements work together to project a central theme. Suppose the idea is to express the aridity of the Grand Canyon. You would choose a view where plant life is sparse and the dominant colors are brown (suggestive of dirt or sand), and a time of day when the sky is free of clouds and the light high in contrast to project a feeling of starkness. No single element in the scene has visual priority by being brighter, sharper, larger, or unique.

Some picture themes are purely visual and have no literal interpretation. They find expression as provocative pattern, beautiful color, or dramatic perspective. It might be a splash of yellow and blue, or an arrangement of ocean waves. Such themes achieve validity through their simple expression of beauty.

Rhythm is one of the more familiar visual themes of landscape photography—the geometric swirl of a mountain stream, a lineup of cottonwoods along a river, or an array of seashells washed onto a beach all have potential for expressing rhythm. Visual rhythm is a repetition of accent and interval, such as ice-capped peaks alternating with blue sky. More interesting rhythms incorporate repetitions of groups of elements, such as groves of aspens scattered over open parkland. Some rhythms suggest movement, such as a row of saguaros arranged smallest to largest.

Frosty Swamp, Yellowstone National Park, Wyoming. *This photograph presents a composition based on a central theme. There is no visual center of interest. Rather the frost, the cool blue-green hues, and the trunks stripped of their bark suggest a frozen solitude.*

Oak Tree, Shenandoah National Park, Virginia. *Although this photograph obviously features a tree, the picture's composition is based on a central theme, one opposite that of the facing image. Equally strong graphic elements create a theme of richness and warmth—the heavily textured, lichen encrusted bark, the fiery colors, the spreading up-reaching limbs, and glowing backlight.*

Balanced Rock at Arches National Park, Utah.
To achieve maximum depth-of-field in this photo, I first set the lens to minimum aperture. Then, with the lens stopped down and my eye to the viewfinder, I adjusted the focus so the scene appeared sharp from the balanced rock formation in the distant background to the dried-out grass in the foreground. At larger apertures and with longer lenses, there would be insufficient depth to include the foreground elements. In such cases, it is necessary to revise the composition so that distracting out-of-focus elements are excluded.

Many of the rhythmic patterns drawn from the landscape need to be strengthened. Should there be an incongruous element in the sequence or pattern, the photographer can eliminate it by a change in the camera angle, lens focal length, or subject magnification to portray a more coherent portion of the pattern. Some rhythms are so regular as to be monotonous—a stand of cattails, for instance. Including a broken cattail in the frame will emphasize the unusual regularity of the pattern and create unexpected irony.

CONTROLLING DEPTH-OF-FIELD

Of the various camera-handling techniques that are used to organize design elements—adjusting camera angle, choosing a film, selecting focal length, etc.—controlling depth-of-field is one of the most important. Depth-of-field is a term that describes the amount of the scene that is in acceptable focus. It is controlled by adjusting the lens aperture. The smaller the aperture, the greater the depth-of-field. Depth-of-field can be precisely evaluated by viewing the scene at the shooting aperture by activating the camera's depth-of-field preview lever.

With landscapes, it is usually desirable that the entire field be rendered sharply. This does not mean, however, that you simply adjust to minimum aperture and begin shooting. Often, maximum depth is possible without using the smallest aperture, allowing you to shoot with mid-range aperture settings which yield the best quality

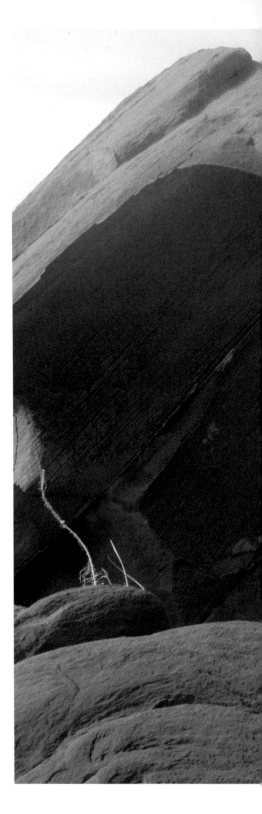

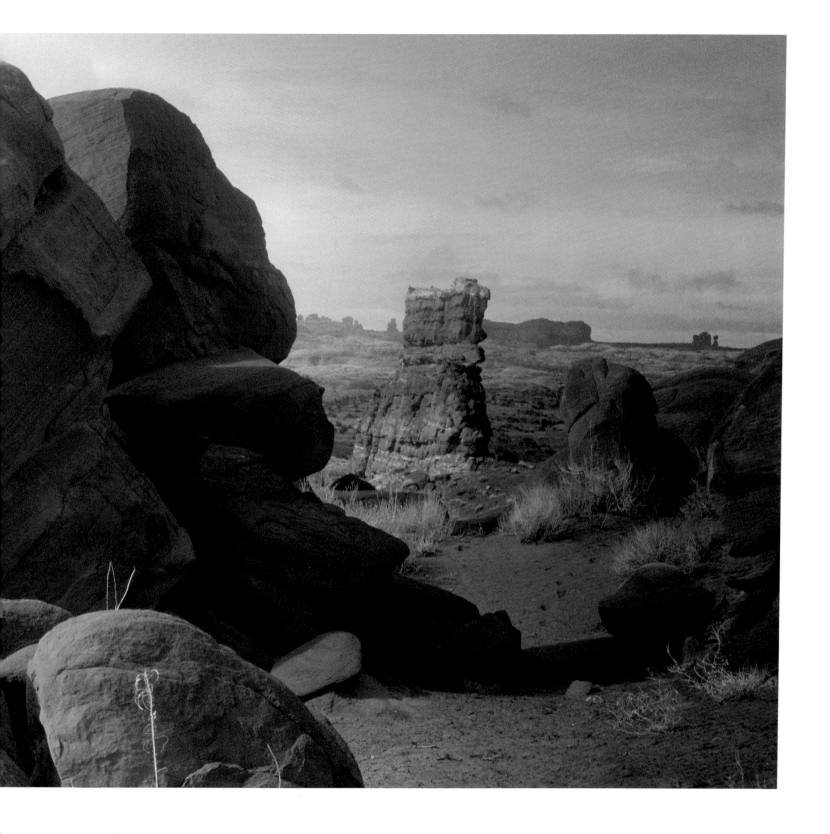

📷 CUSTOM-MADE MOONS *SPECIAL SITUATION*

LANDSCAPE PHOTOGRAPHS which include the moon are best done by double exposure (see your camera's manual for instructions on recording two images on the same frame). This technique allows you to place the moon at any magnification anywhere in the scene. In addition, as the moon and the landscape may vary in brightness by 1,000 times, it allows exposure settings to be customized for each image component.

The moon is photographed at the desired magnification and location within the frame. It should be positioned so that it will fall within a clear portion of the sky (no clouds) in the scene to be photographed subsequently. The moon will seem smaller on film than it does in the viewfinder. A 200 mm lens makes a strong, yet natural, record. Exposure for the moon is the same as for a sunlit subject at midday—some

equivalent of 1/100 second at f/16 with ISO 100 film. In the second exposure, prepare the shot as you would for any landscape. You can change lenses, exposure settings and filtration provided clear sky falls in the same position as the moon. Once everything is set, make the second exposure.

A focusing screen with etched grids is helpful in keeping track of where you recorded the moon. If you are photographing a moon that is less than full, try to match the direction of the lighting on the moon with that on the landscape. For example, if the moon is illuminated on the left side, make sure the landforms are as well. The moon is usually a nighttime phenomenon, and it appears most believable when placed in landscapes photographed at twilight.

resolution. You may also need a larger aperture to allow faster shutter speeds to reduce the movement of elements in the composition, such as windblown foliage.

MAXIMUM DEPTH-OF-FIELD

About 2/3 of the depth-of-field falls behind and 1/3 falls in front of the point at which the lens is focused. In order to make best use of available depth-of-field, it must encompass the most important parts of the scene. This is done by stopping the lens down, studying the relative sharpness of various parts of the scene, and then adjusting the focal distance to position the depth-of-field to best advantage. Maximum depth results when the zone stetches from infinity to some nearer distance. To make sure that the entire field is rendered sharply, frame the scene so that nothing is included that falls in front of the depth-of-field zone.

CONTROLLING PERSPECTIVE

When confronted with a scenic view, you can easily forget that only a small part of what you

North Shore, Lake Superior, Ontario. *Several camera-handling techniques emphasized the feeling of depth in this image: the use of a wide-angle lens positioned close to foreground elements, a camera angle that included similar sized perspective cues (the rock shelves), and making the exposure during a windy period when mist reduced the clarity of distant objects.*

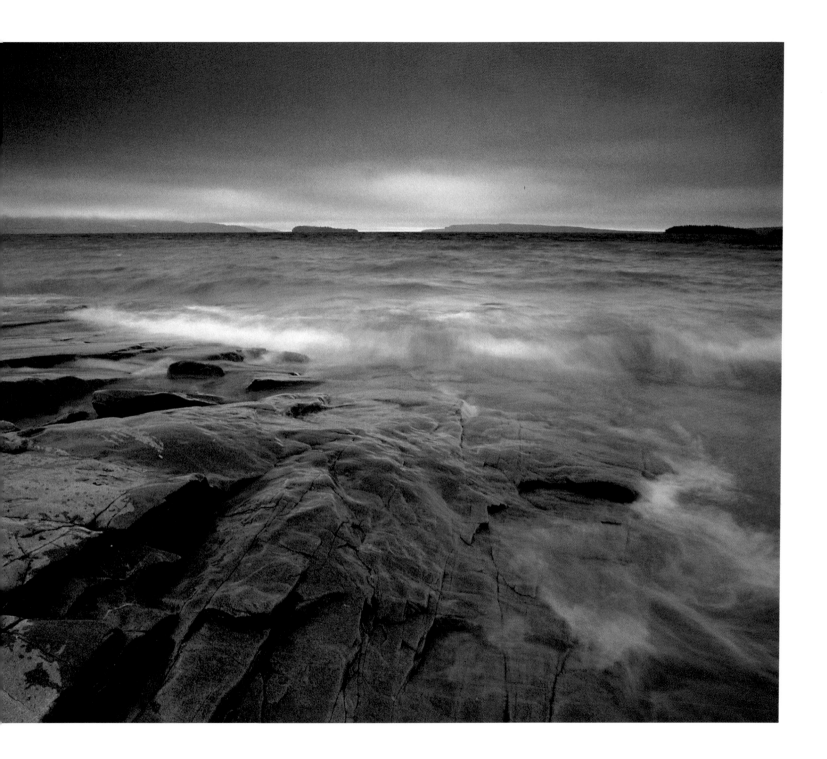

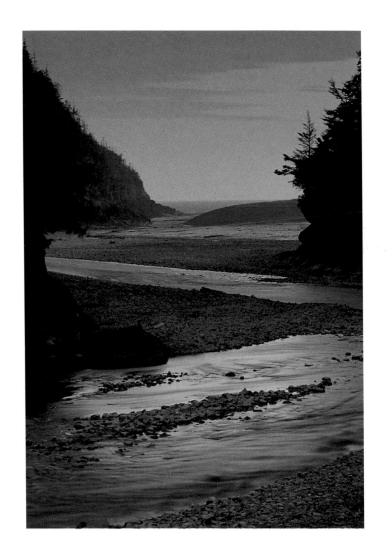

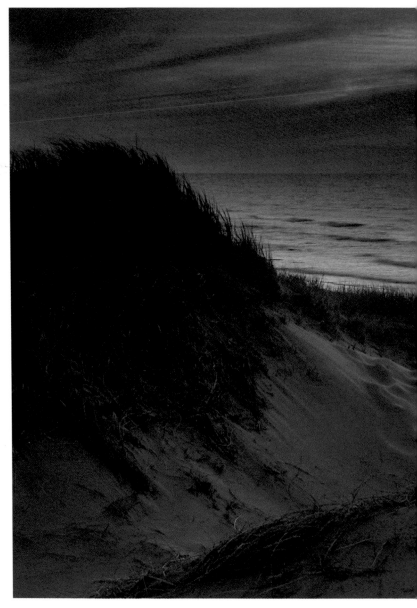

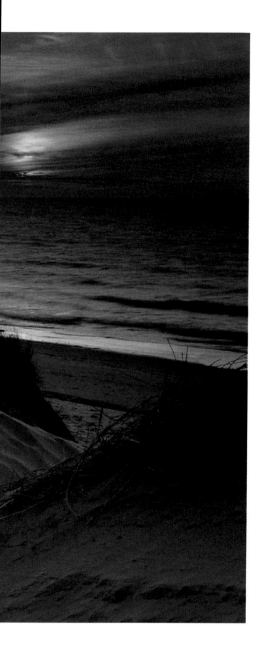

feel is shared by the camera. What you see, you can also hear, smell, and touch—the thunder of surf and scream of a gull, the scent of seaweed and saltwater, and the cool spray of ocean mist. Your eyes play over the scene tirelessly, absorbing its many aspects. However, the 35 mm camera is allowed but a single, frozen view little bigger than a postage stamp. It cannot record the range of light and dark, or the subtle colors that your eyes take for granted. Because it must express three di-mensions on a two-dimensional surface, it is most limited in showing perspective. The spatial rela-tionships described below will help to overcome this shortcoming and infuse the image with a feel-ing of deep space. You may choose to combine contradictory perspective cues to create an ironic impression of simultaneous expansion and con-traction.

The most useful perspective cue is overlap-ping. Features in the landscape that are close to us are in front of those that are farther away. Ma-nipulation of this powerful spatial cue is done by altering the camera position, in most instances laterally, to bring one object in front of another.

Features in the landscape that are near to you are larger than similar ones farther away. The image will express great depth if you include ob-jects in the composition that the viewer assumes are the same size, yet are represented in differing scale in the photograph. Trees are the most com-mon such objects encountered in wilderness habi-tats. Relative size differences of related objects

Fundy National Park, New Brunswick. *The most significant perspective cue in this image is the river receding into the distance, its width growing smaller as each bend in the stream comes into view. Taken about 15 minutes after sundown, the photo exhibits a violet color cast due to the color of the evening twilight and the long exposure (30 seconds) which caused a color shift in the film emulsion.*

Prince Edward Island National Park. *As with most photographs in which the sun is included in the composition, it was necessary to reduce the sky's brilliance by use of a variable neutral density filter.*

can be strengthened by using a wide-angle lens, and reduced by using a telephoto lens.

Because we view the landscape from five or six feet above the ground, features close to us are situated lower in the scene than those farther away. If your intent is to show depth, position the camera so that it is higher than the foreground objects.

Due mostly to atmospheric haze, close objects appear sharper than ones farther away. This is called aerial perspective. It is most obvious when the atmosphere is loaded with suspended particles, such as found in humid environments, or during periods of fog, mist, rain, snow, or dust. These conditions are so common that photographs that show little aerial perspective because they were made at high elevations, or where the air is dry and still, take on a surreal effect.

Sidelighting emphasizes the contours of the land. It makes features that are important size cues easier to identify and compare. The overlapping of objects or landscape planes is emphasized because the shadow portion of one object is set against the highlight portion of another.

FIELD ROUTINES

With experience, you will develop shooting routines which make you more productive. For beginners, it is helpful to devise some basic procedures, rather than wait for them to grow by trial and error. Following are the steps that I follow most of the time when working in the field. You can adapt them to your particular needs.

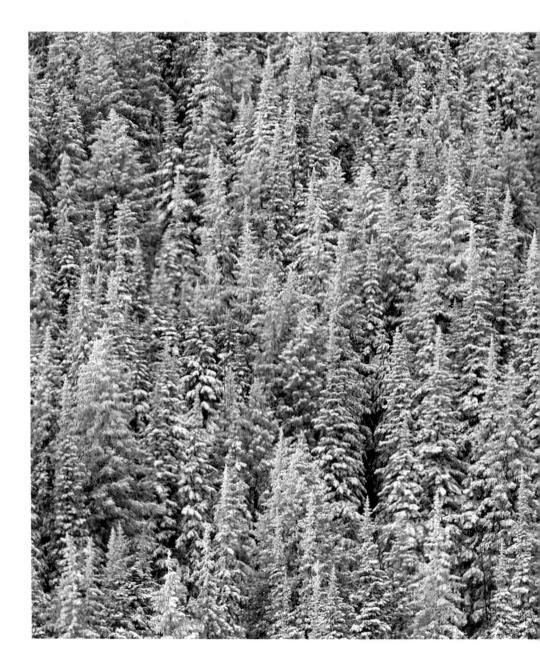

80

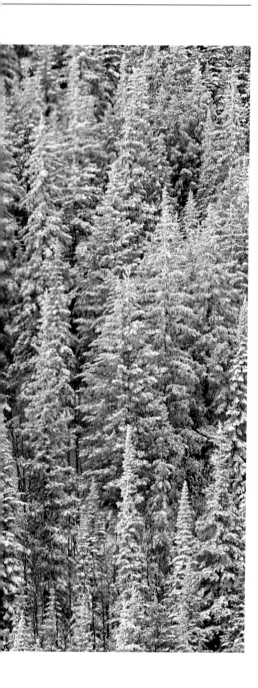

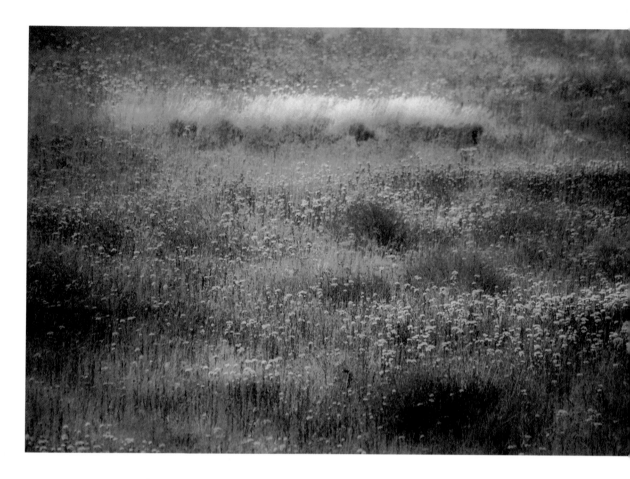

Alpine Forest, Santa Fe National Forest, New Mexico. *The use of a 300 mm lens has flattened the perspective in this photo by eliminating differences in size and detail. However, perspective is still suggested due to the overlapping of trees, resulting in a surreal effect.*

Autumn Meadow, Pennsylvania. *The glow which seems to emanate from this meadow was achieved by photographing the scene twice and sandwiching the two slides together. One image was made at maximum depth-of-field and the other was made with the lens focused in front of the scene to create blur. Each frame was overexposed by one stop so that when the images were sandwiched, correct density would result.*

A DAY OF SHOOTING

When working away from home, I am in position, ready to shoot about one half hour before sunrise. Sometimes I work from the side of the road, at other times I hike into the location. I have already scouted the area the day before, and I have specific plans about where I will setup and the types of photos I hope to make. I carry two cameras, a tripod (sometimes two), lenses from 18 mm to 300 mm, lots of filters, and at least ten rolls of film. I shoot in this location, and sometimes others nearby, until the light fails, usually about an hour after sunup. If there is fog or mist, the shooting period could be considerably longer. As I make my way back to camp, I keep my eyes open for unexpected opportunities.

I spend the rest of the morning eating, and taking care of camping chores. I prepare the film I shot that morning for mailing. I review various travel guides and maps of the area in preparation for the afternoon's scouting expedition. I spend

Sunset at Clingman's Dome, Great Smoky Mountains National Park, North Carolina. There are numerous exciting look-outs in this national park accessible by car, and of course, countless others that are reached by hiking. When shooting in the evening when the sky is clear, keep in mind that the most attractive light often occurs after the sun has set. Although exposure times may be measured in minutes, rather than seconds, contrast in the scene is reduced, allowing better detail in both highlight and shadow areas.

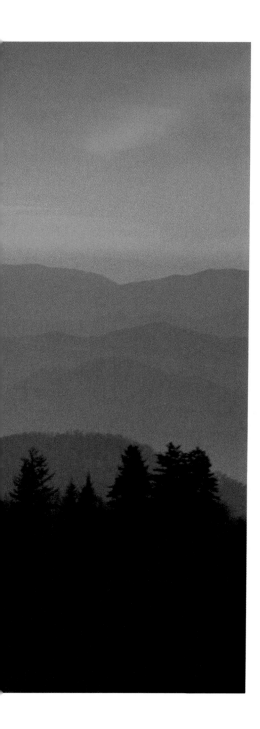

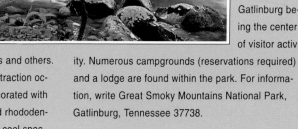 GREAT SMOKY MOUNTAINS *SCENIC HOTSPOT*

THE MOST popular national park in the United States, Great Smoky Mountains National Park lies at the southern terminus of the Appalachian range. Photographers are drawn to the mist-shrouded ridges, streams, waterfalls, and hardwood forests which spread across half a million acres of reclaimed wilderness. Due to heavy rain, trees of numerous species grow larger here than anywhere else in North America. Spring and fall are the preferred seasons for photography. In May the forest floor is spread with wildflowers—trilliums, trout lilies, bluets and others. However, the more noteworthy floral attraction occurs in June. The hillsides become decorated with the pink and white blooms of laurel and rhododendron shrubs, a beautiful contrast to the cool spectrum of forest greens. In autumn, the roads are filled with cars—leaf-lookers (as they are called by the locals) out to see the display of color, and photographers set on recording it on film. The Smokies support the greatest variety of trees east of the Mississippi and this is reflected in the forest's autumn palette. Knoxville, Tennessee is a couple of hour's drive from the park. Accommodation of all types is offered in communities near the park, with Gatlinburg being the center of visitor activity. Numerous campgrounds (reservations required) and a lodge are found within the park. For information, write Great Smoky Mountains National Park, Gatlinburg, Tennessee 37738.

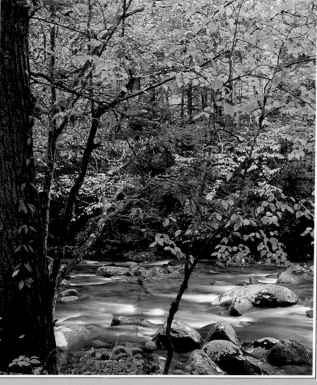

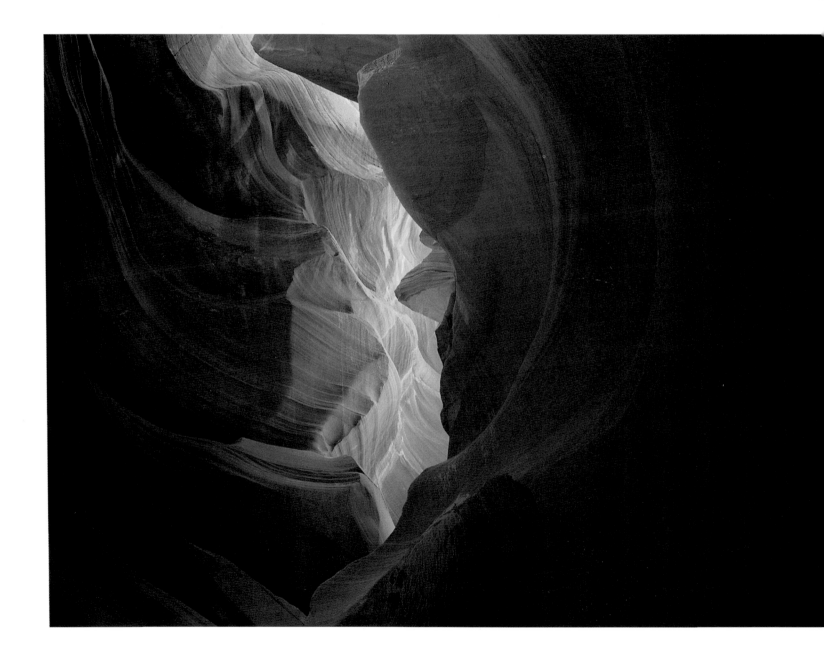

the afternoon checking out new locations for the evening shooting session, and for the next morning as well. I don't carry any equipment to do this, which is a relief and about the only time I can truly enjoy hiking. I eat a big lunch about three o'clock so that I have lots of energy for the upcoming shoot. The evening's photography goes about the same as the morning's except I work as long as one half hour after sundown. If I have had an easy day, I will set up the tripod to take some star or moon pictures after dark. But usually, I'm too tired and I go to bed early.

SHOOTING A LANDSCAPE

I have more specific routines for actually shooting. Once I have reached the location, I may wander around briefly testing different views with my eye to the viewfinder. Once I have settled on a shot, I set up the tripod and mount the camera.
Framing. The first step is to precisely frame the scene by changing the camera angle and adjusting the focal length of the zoom lens until I have the right magnification.
Depth-of-field. Next I set the depth-of-field by stopping down the lens and, with my eye to the viewfinder, adjusting the aperture and focus.
Polarizing Filter. Usually there is a polarizing filter on the lens so I rotate it until I like the effect, usually this is at maximum polarization. If there is no change in the effect, I know the filter is unnecessary and I remove it.
Contrast Control Filters. If the scene is high in

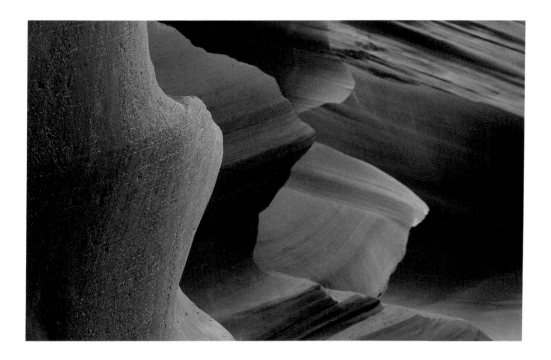

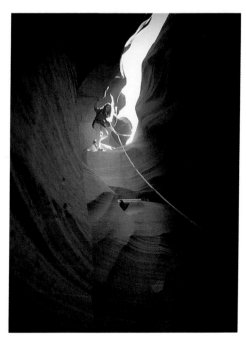

Antelope Slot Canyon, Arizona. *These beautiful subterranean rock formations, found near Page, Arizona, offer great opportunity to create abstract compositions. Unlike other landscape subjects, they are best photographed during the brightest part of the day due to the canyon's narrow opening which throws most of the interior into deep shade. A tripod is essential as exposures usually exceed several seconds at small apertures.*

85

📷 STORMY WEATHER *SPECIAL SITUATION*

FILM IS unable to record rain or snow effectively except under optimum conditions of light and camera angle. A camera position which places the precipitation against a dark background is necessary.

Sidelighting or backlighting will illuminate the rain or snow and simultaneously throw the background into shadow, creating the required contrast. Underexposing the scene a stop may also serve to emphasize the rain or snow. Precipitation can be further distinguished by double exposure. Under-expose the first image by one stop. Re-focus on the raindrops or snowflakes that are falling closer to you to make them appear larger, and record the second image, again under exposing by one stop.

Lightning happens too quickly to record by manual release of the shutter. Instead adjust the aperture for a one or two minute exposure. (Neutral density filters may be necessary if conditions are bright.) Aim the camera at the area of most electrical activity and open the shutter when you see the first bolt. Another flash will usually occur within 30 seconds in the same spot. To re-cord multiple lightning tracks, keep the shutter open (use the bulb setting), and carefully block light from the lens during intervals between flashes with your hat or a dark cloth. Don't jar the camera during the exposure. With this technique, you can record all the lightning that occurs over a period of an hour or two on one frame without over exposure.

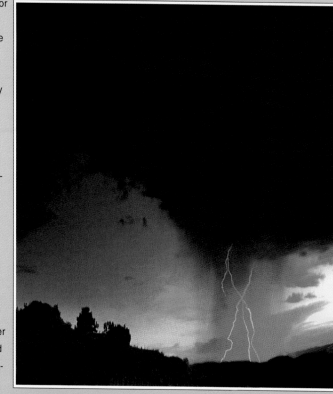

contrast (a near certainty if the sky is included in the composition), I mount graduated neutral density filters of different densities until contrast is acceptable. Sometimes, I might try a color filter to see how it affects the scene. It's not unusual for me to shoot with four different filters on the lens.

Exposure. Once the filtration is set, I take a light meter reading and set the shutter speed for the correct exposure.

Viewfinder Check. Before I start making exposures, I make a last check of the viewfinder to ensure everything is perfect. I look especially for out-of-focus branches or grass which might be poking into the edge of the composition.

Controlling Flare. I shade the lens with my hat (there are too many filters to use a lens hood) to prevent direct sunlight from striking the filters or the front lens element and creating flare.

Shooting and Bracketing. Finally, using the remote electric shutter release, I begin shooting: ten frames at the priority exposure, seven at 1/2 stop higher, seven at 1/2 stop lower, then another four photos each at a further 1/2 stop higher and 1/2 stop lower.

Shiprock, New Mexico. *This great stone monolith dominates the skyline of northeastern New Mexico. I have photographed its sculptured form often, in different light and weather conditions. Like most landscapes, it shows a different face to my camera each time I visit. It isn't persistence that provokes my return, for I have no need of more photos. I enjoy it.*

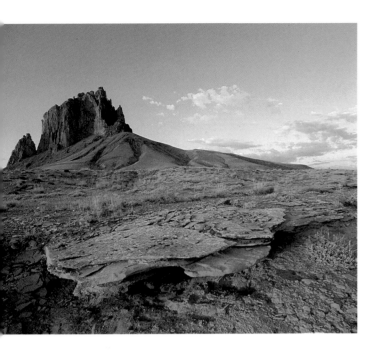

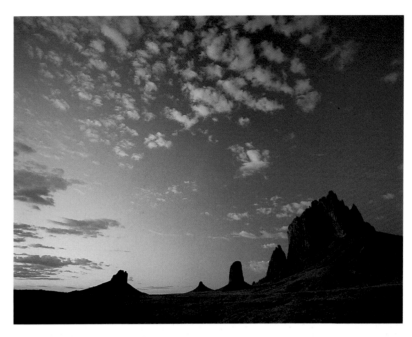

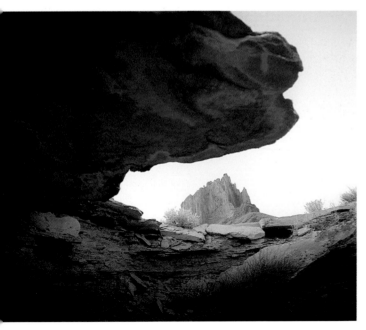

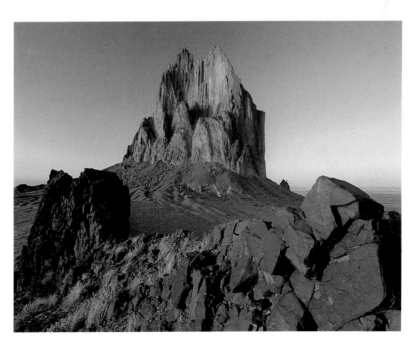

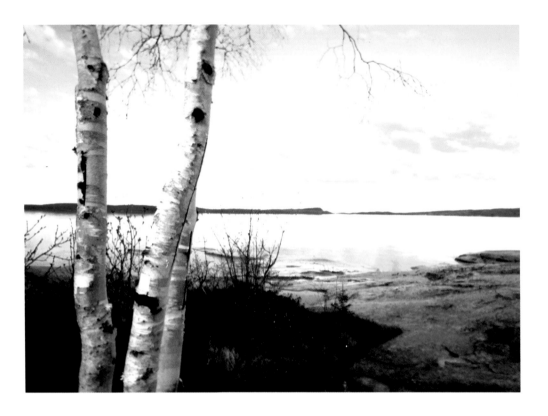

Lake of the Woods, Ontario. *Taken on a bright, overcast day, the trees in this photo exhibited good color and detail, but they were overshadowed by the expanse of white sky and its reflection in the lake. To correct the problem, I scanned the image using a desktop scanner, the Nikon Coolscan, transcribing its color pigments into digital informatiion that I subsequently manipulated on a Macintosh computer. I used a photograph editing software program called Adobe Photoshop to add color to the sky and its reflection in the lake. The image was later converted back to film for reproduction in this book.*

Verticals. If it suits the scene, I switch to a vertical format and repeat the entire exposure regime. Most of the time, there is another variation on the composition which I would like to try (usually it involves a change in magnification) and I repeat the entire procedure again before calling it quits.

ELECTRONIC COMPOSITION

Advances in personal computer technology have made it possible for amateur photographers to manipulate their images using a variety of software. Not only can traditional darkroom techniques such as dodging and burning be carried out on the monitor with a few clicks of the mouse, but the photographer can also add and manipulate colors, paint and draw on the image, and combine selected elements of two or more slides into one composition. In fact, the only limitation is the photographer's imagination.

Photographic images can be converted into digital computer images with a desktop scanner, or you can send your slides to Kodak to have them scanned onto a compact disk (CD ROM) at minimal cost. You can then edit and manipulate the image at leisure. The new image can be viewed on your monitor or printed on a color printer. Printer output varies from poor to photographic quality.

Creating images on the computer is great fun. The results are as convincing as those of conventional photography. This technology frees the photographer from working with some of the cumbersome aspects of camera and chemical emul-

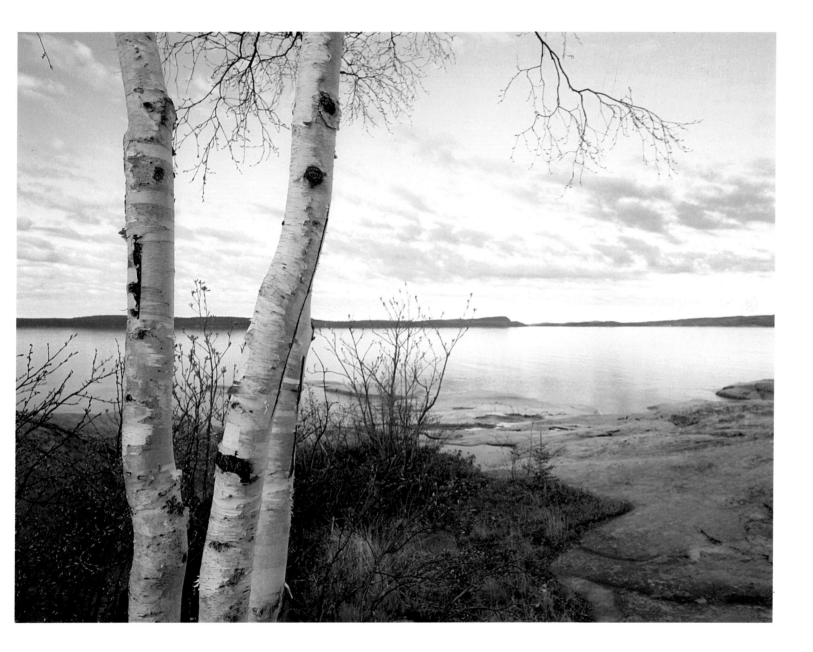

Rising Moon over Jasper National Park, Alberta. *Although the digital darkroom is an efficient and precise method of carrying out traditional photographic procedures, such as dodging and burning to correct image flaws, its significant impact on photography is to create a radically more expressive art form. When done skillfully, it can create an illusion of reality as convincing as traditional photographic techniques. It can also be used to create powerful images that are bound only by the photographer's imagination. To make this image, I collected the components of a number of slides by scanning each photograph, and then, using Adobe Photoshop software, combined them in the new composition.*

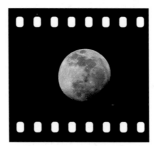

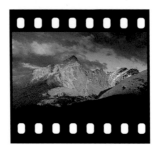

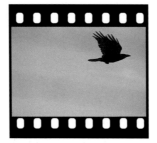

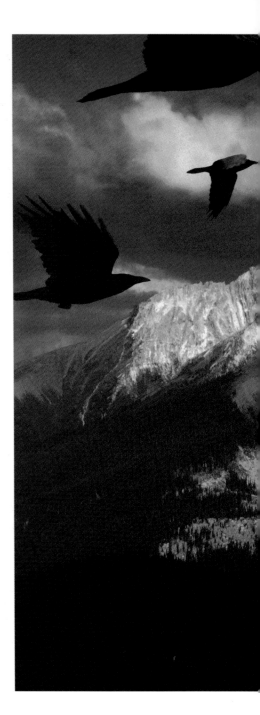

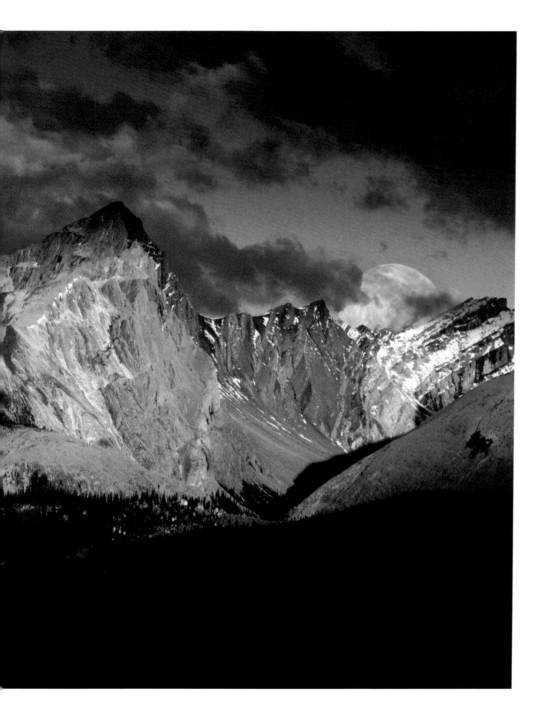

sions, and offers as much spontaneity and freedom in creating images as that enjoyed by painters. At the same time, it places new artistic and technological demands on the photographer.

The magic that transforms a photograph into art cannot be practised or learned. Ultimately it is a product of the photographer's genius as an individual, a reflection of his own personality. Where and how you chose to point the camera will be colored by your personality and experience. As an aspiring photographer, you should understand that the way you see a winter forest or a mountain meadow is unique, and therefore of potential artistic value.

91

PART IV

Selling Photographs

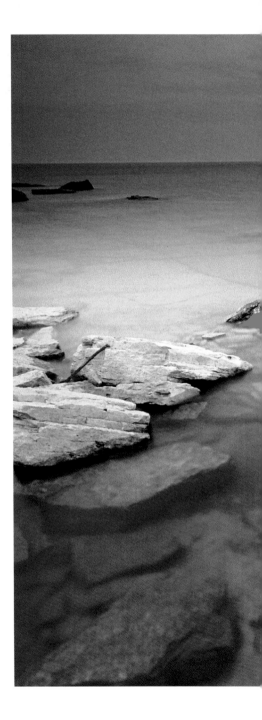

THE SUPPORT OF editors and art directors as picture publishers helps under-write the expense of landscape photography. These photo buyers must satisfy the desires of the people who support their publications. Only a few are in a position to publish photography that attempts to formulate public taste.

There are two basic approaches to selling your work. The simplest and most direct way is to sell your photographs as art prints. The more lucrative way is to sell only the rights to your work to picture publishers of various types.

ART PRINTS

A lot of scenic photographers, even professional ones, make prints from their trans-parencies to sell as display art. The best prints are made directly (no inter-negative stage) on Cibachrome printing paper. Many photographers with darkrooms make their own Cibachrome prints. The process is simple and fun. You can also have your slides printed at a custom lab.

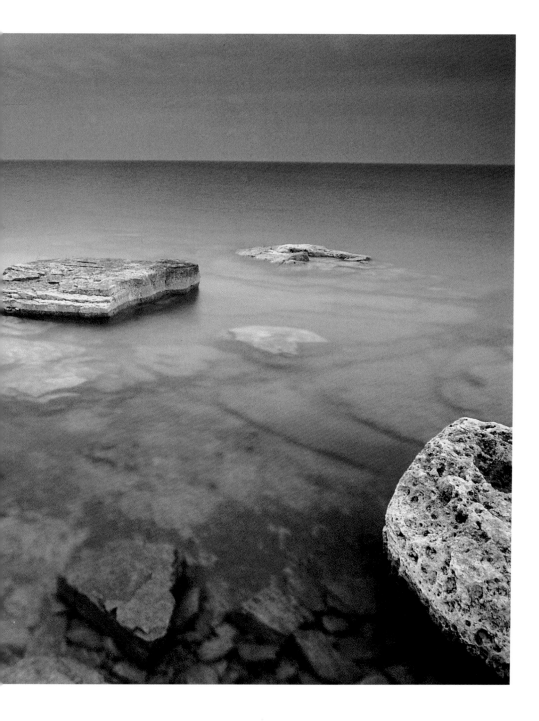

Georgian Bay, Ontario. *This photo is my best selling art print. The monochromatic color, unusual lighting, and low, wide-angle perspective give it an abstract, mysterious quality. At the same time, the cool pastel tones and pleasing shapes are comforting. If you have a blue sofa, it's perfect. For most photographers, art prints provide only supplemental income. A local gallery has sold 15 of these prints (as limited editions) in two years, each at about the price of a good tripod.*

Columbia Mountains, British Columbia. *The ease with which photographs can be made sustains a general belief that photography is not a fine art medium. When selecting photographs from your collection for the art print market, this prejudice can be side-stepped by choosing photographs that resemble paintings. Abstract images readily fit this category. I used a telephoto lens to isolate this view from customary references to perspective, form, scale, and color, thereby diminishing the reality of the scene.*

Salton Sea National Wildlife Refuge, California. *Limiting the color in a photograph is an easy way to create an abstract image likely to find acceptance in the art print market. Careful framing, a telephoto lens, and the calm of early morning resulted in a dream-like mood.*

The prints should be loosely hung (not dry-mounted) on acid-free mount board, matted, and shrink-wrapped by a professional framing shop. Leave it to the buyer to complete the job with a frame of his choice—the most expensive part of preparing a print for display.

You can show prints to your friends, acquaintances, and business associates personally. Restaurants and banks often have wall space for hanging art. It brings in customers so it is usually offered to artists without cost. Your telephone number is made available to people interested in your work, and it is up to you to complete the deal. It isn't necessary to pay a commission.

It feels good to see your photos hanging in an art gallery, but it's not easy to convince a dealer to devote space to your work. With a private gallery, I sometimes appear unannounced with a bundle of prints at a time when the dealer is likely to have a few spare minutes to talk with me—early weekday afternoons are best. Concentrate on galleries that handle artwork similar to yours in subject matter, aesthetic approach, and price. Art dealers take a 50% commission, and you pay for the printing and framing out of your share. I know of few living scenic photographers who have made much more than pocket money doing this. However, the experience is fun and a good way to meet interesting people that share your interest in art.

Another way to sell your prints is at an arts and craft fair. There are thousands of such events

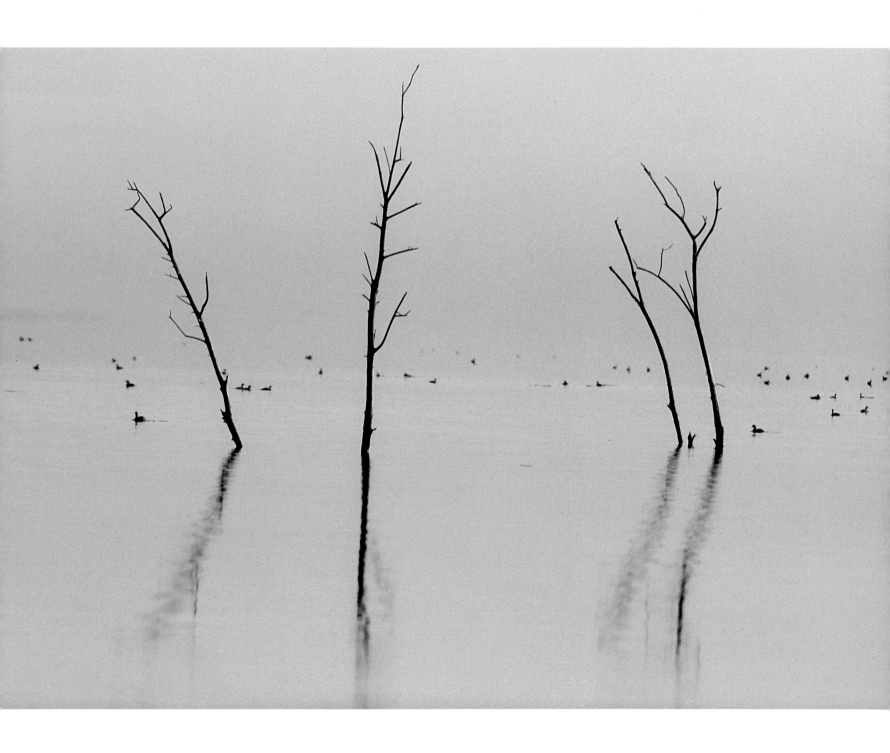

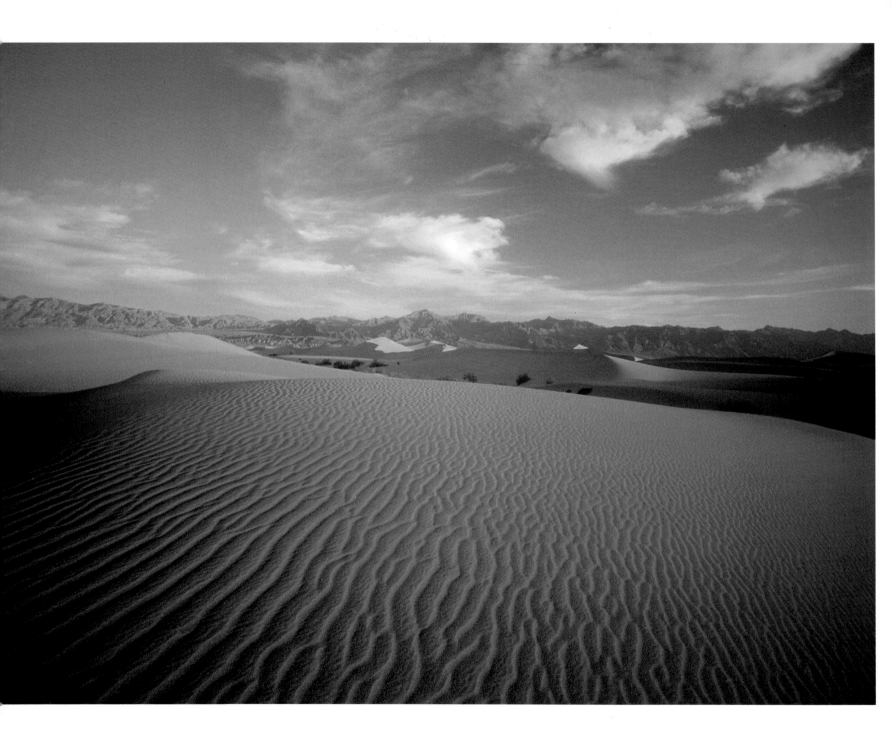

throughout North America each year. You rent a space for a few days, set up a makeshift gallery, and wait for the rush of customers. Again, these are exciting social events, but the profits seldom amount to much.

PICTURE PUBLISHERS

Magazine and calendar publishers buy one-time rights to reproduce your photograph. The picture is returned as soon as the printing is completed, and you are free to sell the rights again to another publisher. Exceptional images can sell hundreds of times. One-time rights are usually purchased for $100 to $200, or more, depending on the publication. Transactions are commonly done by mail.

MAGAZINES

Contacting magazine picture buyers is easy. Within the first few pages of every magazine, you will find a list of the people who produce it. Look for the photo or illustrations editor, or failing this, the art director. Send this person a set of 20 or 40

Sand Dunes, Death Valley National Monument, California. *Sidelight from a setting sun clearly shows the textured surface of these dunes. The pattern draws the eye into the scene, and its diminishing scale creates an impression of three dimensions. I used a polarizing filter to darken the sky and a variable neutral density filter to darken the foreground dunes, further emphasizing the central region of the image.*

📷 **GRAND TETON NATIONAL PARK**   *SCENIC HOTSPOT*

THE GRAND TETON Mountains are widely acknowledged as the most inspiring peaks in the Rockies. Jagged spires that rise abruptly 7,500 feet out of the flat, broad Jackson Hole Valley, they are the classic mountains of the American West. For landscape photographers, the attraction is doubled by the numerous quiet lakes and river backwaters that reflect, with mirror-like precision, the great ice-capped monuments. Grand Teton National Park is a haven for elk, deer, buffalo, and especially moose. There is ample opportunity to incorporate wildlife into scenic compositions. In early summer, it is possible to photograph the mountains with a foreground of yellow sunflowers, blue lupines and scarlet gilia which carpet the valley floor. By August, the blooms move upward into the alpine areas and so do photographers. Autumn is the most popular shooting season due to the color of the aspens, oaks, and cottonwoods which illuminate the hillsides and river valleys.

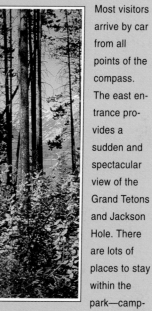

The main road through the park is kept open through the winter when clear blue skies, interrupted occasionally by dramatic storms, lure photographers to a landscape transformed by snow.

Most visitors arrive by car from all points of the compass. The east entrance provides a sudden and spectacular view of the Grand Tetons and Jackson Hole. There are lots of places to stay within the park—campsites, cabins, and lodges only minutes from the best scenic locations, as well as private lodgings in the town of Jackson. Grand Teton National Park shares its northern border with Yellowstone National Park. For information, write Grand Teton National Park, P.O. Box 170, Moose, Wyoming 83012.

duplicates of your best photographs, particularly those likely to be used in the magazine. Include a list of subjects in your files, and a request that the editor advise you of future photographic needs. This is usually done by a periodic mailing of a 'wants' list to a select group of photographers.

CALENDARS

The biggest buyers, by far, of scenic photography are calendar publishers. There are hundreds of them, and some publish 25 or more scenic titles each year. To find out who they are, visit large bookstores in the fall and check out their calendar selection. Copy down the name and location of the companies you think would be interested in your work. Call the company and get their full mailing address and the name of their

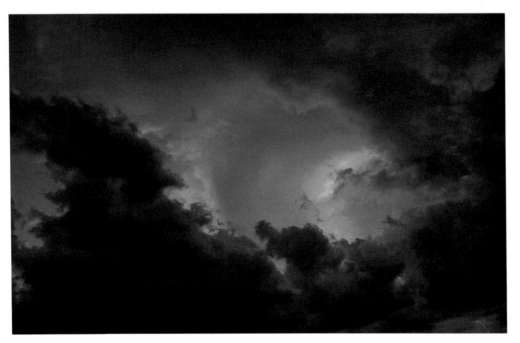

Surf on Rocks. *Pictures expressing concepts, such as freedom, adventure, or joy, are most in demand by photo agencies. Their clients are advertisers looking for images that evoke an emotional response. This photo might be used to sell soap, or better, the value of clean oceans. An exposure of 1/4 second, timed to catch a breaking wave, resulted in the smooth water pattern.*

Cloud Formations. *As celestial phenomena, clouds can be used to illustrate many religious and spiritual concepts. A dramatic skyscape can sell hundreds of times if placed with a professional agency. I used a telephoto lens to isolate these colorful formations.*

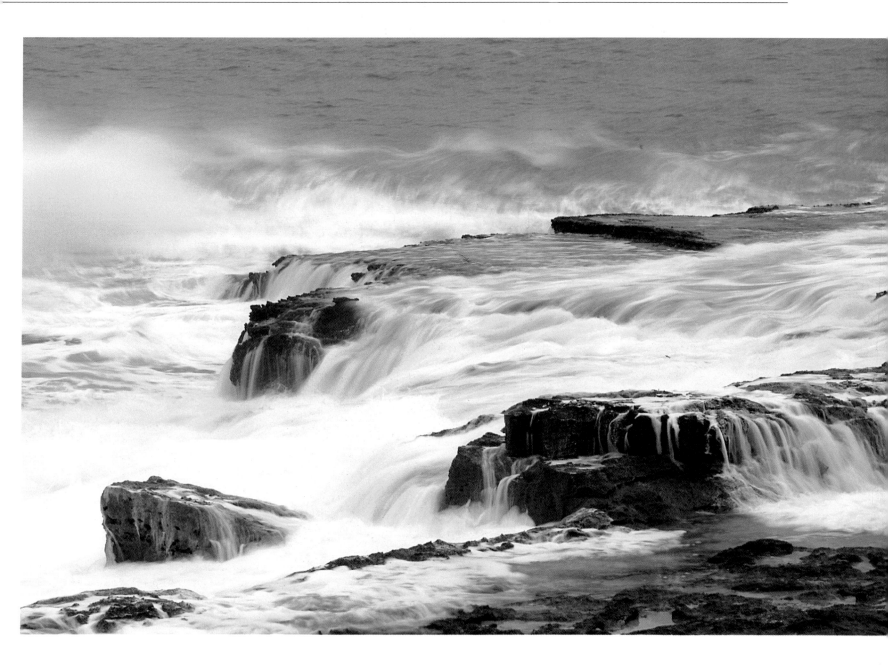

picture buyer. Then query the buyer in the same manner described above for magazines.

The great thing about calendar companies is that most of them are interested in ideas for new calendars. If you have a good idea and the photographs to back it up, you can submit a selection of images for an entire calendar—topics such as 'Sunrise at the Grand Canyon', 'Wild Rivers of America', or 'Pacific Shores'. I work continually on a dozen themes at once. Twenty pictures are sufficient to sell the proposal, but remember that you need to supply pictures to illustrate each season. Otherwise, the project will fail.

Some calendar companies pay upon acceptance, but most pay on publication which is in the summer or fall preceding the year of the calendar. The best time to submit photos is during the spring and summer. These will be considered for calendars to be published two years later.

PICTURE AGENCIES

You might wonder about handing over your photos to a picture agency, and letting it take

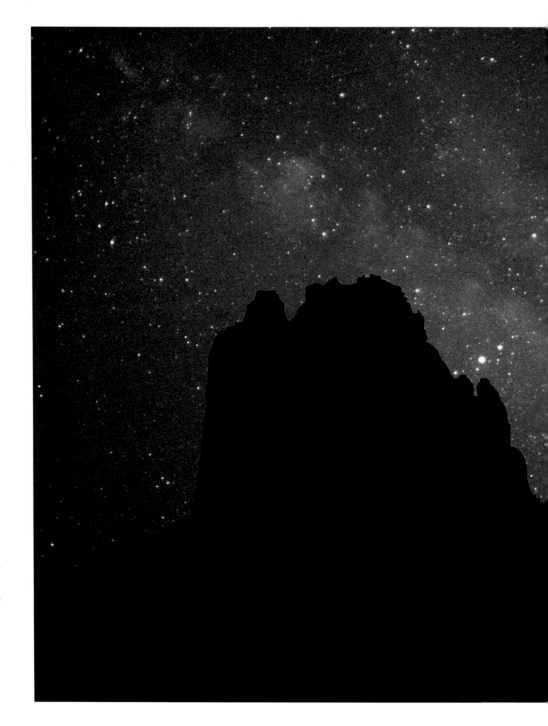

Starry Night at Shiprock, New Mexico. This photograph was made in two stages. First I photographed the rock silhouetted against a bright sky a few minutes after sundown. I overexposed the sky by two stops to wash out all the color and detail. Later I sandwiched this slide with a picture of the heavens taken, coincidentally, in the same spot using an equatorial sky tracker (see inset).

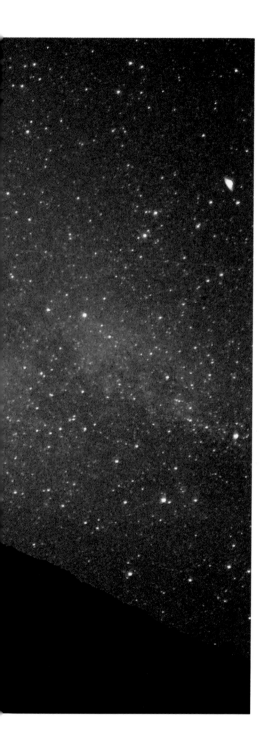

📷 STARSCAPES *SPECIAL SITUATION*

STARS ARE usually photographed as trails of light arcing across the heavens. Like the sun, their apparent movement is due to the rotation of the earth. The technique is simple. You frame a portion of the sky and make a time-exposure of one hour, or more, using fine-grained film with the lens wide open. Don't worry about overexposure as long as it is completely dark. Photographs of star trails are more appealing if you include interesting foreground elements (trees or landforms) which will appear as silhouettes.

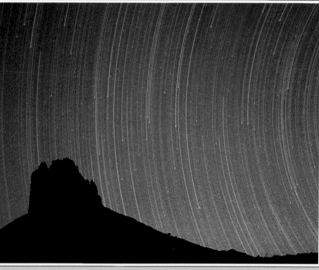

Further interest can be added to star trails by showing the warm glow of the sky near the horizon that occurs after the sun has set. Take a spot-meter reading of this area and then underexpose by one stop. Expose the same frame again (a double exposure) once it is dark and the stars are visible.

To photograph the stars as we see them, as pinpoints of light scattered through the heavens, a high speed film of ISO 1000 is necessary. Set the lens at maximum aperture and try exposures from 5 to 30 seconds. At longer exposures, the stars will start to leave trails. For images on fine-grained film, you need a star tracker, a device that keeps the lens trained on a field of stars by continually repositioning the camera as the earth rotates. The tracker is aligned with the earth's axis by sighting on Polaris (the North Star) which hangs above the North Pole, and appears not to move. The camera, which is mounted on top of the tracker, can frame up any part of the heavens using any lens. Exposures of two or three hours (at maximum aperture) can be made without blurring. Because the camera is moving, sharply rendered foreground elements cannot be included in the composition. They must be recorded on another frame as silhouettes against a light background and then sandwiched with the starscape. For information on purchasing a star tracker, consult Edward R. Byers Co., 29001 West Highway 58, Barstow, California 92311.

Micro-landscapes. *Close-up photographs of the landscape are chosen by editors to symbolize a region or season. Specialized equipment is not needed. All of these photos were taken with a telephoto zoom lens with macro-focusing capability, a standard feature on such lenses. For the most professional results, shoot on overcast days when the light is soft, lightly dampen the scene with a fine mist to create saturated color, and use a polarizer to eliminate reflections. If you rearrange objects to improve the composition, remember that the scene must look natural to be convincing.*

care of the selling. Unfortunately picture agencies are inundated with requests for representation from aspiring photographers. Many of them are currently reducing the number of photographers they work with to a select group of top producers. You needn't consider an agency until you have at least 500 exceptional images to place in their files. Agencies keep one half of whatever they sell.

PREPARING SUBMISSIONS

You seldom meet or even get to speak with picture editors, so there is no need to develop a convincing sales pitch. Your photographs must do all the talking for you. When you are assembling slides for a submission, be critical. If in doubt about a photo's merit, set it aside. If you are presenting a portfolio to gain inclusion on a mailing list, submit only full sheets of slides, that is multiples of 20, rather than 23 or 37, which will lead the reviewer to think you sent in every decent slide in your collection. You want the editor to think that there are a lot more great images stored in your files. Each slide must be labeled with your name, a copyright symbol, and the year it was taken, as well as the location of the scene.

If you have a personal computer, you can save a lot of time and give your slides a professional look by using a slide labeling program. These programs are written for use with Avery self-adhesive labels. Several brands of software are advertised regularly in photography magazines. I use Cradoc Caption Writer.

Once the slide is labeled, insert it in a clear, individual slide sleeve to protect it from the careless handling it may receive before you see it again. These individual protectors are made by the Kimac Company. Then place the transparencies in clear, letter-size slide sheets so that the editor can conveniently view 20 slides at a time. Use sheets that do not obscure the caption printed on the bottom of the slide mount. Arrange the slides for maximum visual impact, as you might arrange them for a gallery exhibition. When placing slides in a sheet, I alternate warm and cool colored pictures so that each image is emphasized by contrast with its neighbor.

Attach a covering letter with the submission, and keep careful records of what you send where. I send all domestic submissions by certified mail and international shipments by registered mail. First-time submissions should be accompanied by a S.A.S.E. (self-addressed, stamped envelope). Once you are on the mailing list, subsequent submissions are returned at the expense of the publisher unless you are informed otherwise. Call about ten days after you post the package to find out how your submission is being handled and when you might expect it back.

SHOOTING STRATEGIES

The process of selling photographs for publication is straightforward. The key to success is to take exceptionally good photographs and show them to as many editors as possible. Despite your

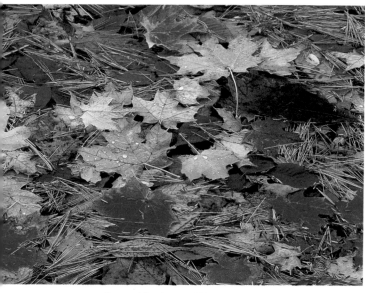

Sugar Maple and White Pine Woodlands, Quebec.

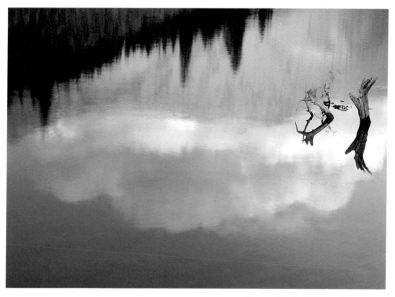

Alpine Reflections, Colorado.

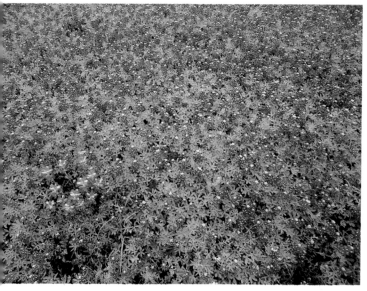

Bluebonnets and Paintbrushes, Texas Hill Country.

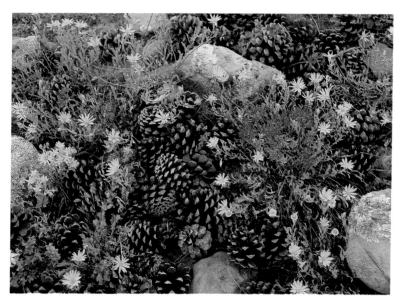

Ponderosa Pine Woodlands, Arizona.

📷 GRAND CANYON NATIONAL PARK *SCENIC HOTSPOT*

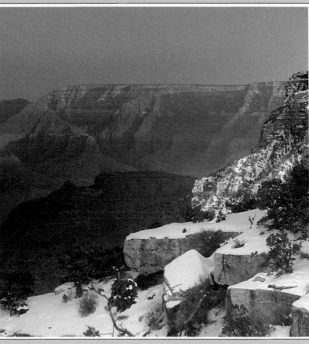

MORE THAN 3,000 feet deep, the Grand Canyon's attraction to photographers is its unbelievable scale and the many spectacular overlooks. The east/west orientation of the canyon embraces both early morning and evening light, illuminating the rock formations, to produce an ever-changing panorama of sculpted forms. The rocks themselves are of many different colors, and these rich hues intensify when dampened by rain.

The Grand Canyon provides many photographic possibilties at any time of the year. The crowds are never so great as to prevent enjoyable photography. Clouds are most spectacular late in the summer when thunderstorms punctuate the day's end. Skies are also dramatic during the winter when the contours of the canyons, cliffs, and rock towers are outlined by snow. The South Rim offers the most shooting locations, but the North Rim also has many attractions. It receives twice as much rain as the South Rim and is covered with spruce and pine forests. Havasu Falls, on the Havasupi Indian Reservation at the southwestern end of the canyon, is one of the most beautiful waterfalls in the world. It is seldom photographed because it is accessible only by horseback or foot. If you are flying, Flagstaff will be your jump-off destination. It's about 90 miles by car from the Grand Canyon. The route takes you through the Painted Desert where the empty landscape is enlivened by colorful rock strata well worth photographing. Accommodation is limited to campsites, cabins, and lodges found inside the national park. For information, write to Grand Canyon National Park, P.O. Box 129, Grand Canyon, Arizona 86023.

best intentions, many of your photos won't make the grade, especially when you are just starting. Wilderness photography has thousands of devoted adherents and all but the very best photographs are rejected for publication. Following are some specific recommendations for taking landscape photographs that sell.

Shoot when the sun nears the horizon. The light at these times is invariably more attractive than at midday. Get started at least an hour before sun-up. Scout out good locations duriing midday and save your film for the best light. Be especially aware of the delicate light that occurs for ten or twenty minutes after the sun has set.

Shoot popular subjects. Photographs of well known scenic attractions in national parks have the widest market appeal. Not only do these landscapes produce dramatic imagery but they satisfy demands for pictures of wilderness and nature, characteristic state or national landmarks, and the national park itself.

Use a polarizer. Many photographers are not aware of the extra color saturation that is achieved by using a polarizing filter. The aim is

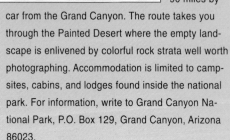

Waterton Lakes National Park, Alberta. The mountainside in the background of this photo lies in the shade and is illuminated only by light reflected from the blue sky overhead. Although our eyes compensate for the cool color cast, it is recorded objectively by film. Shaded backgrounds provide dramatic contrast for backlit translucent subjects such as these leaves.

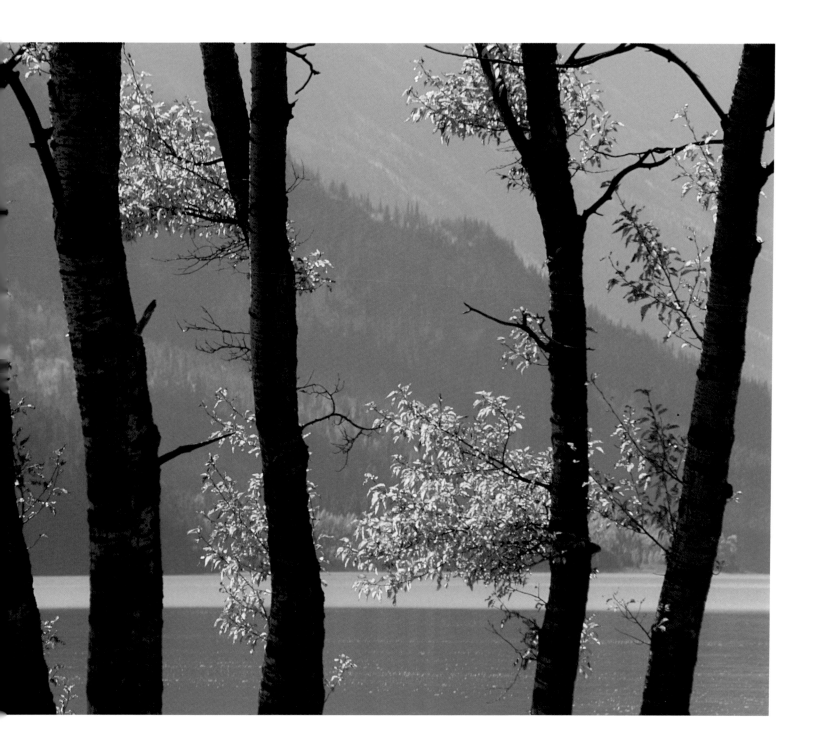

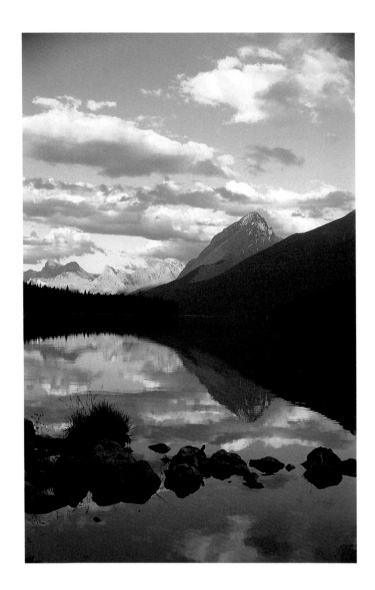

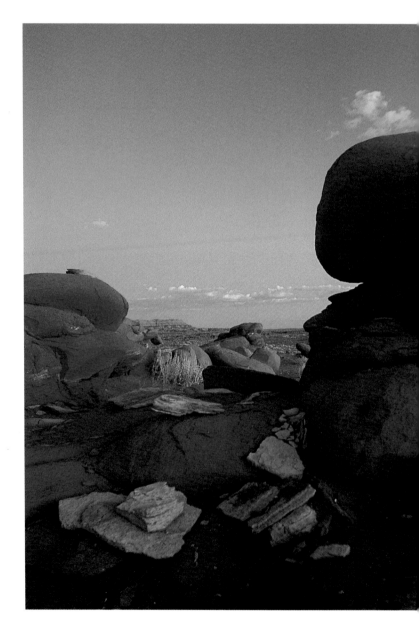

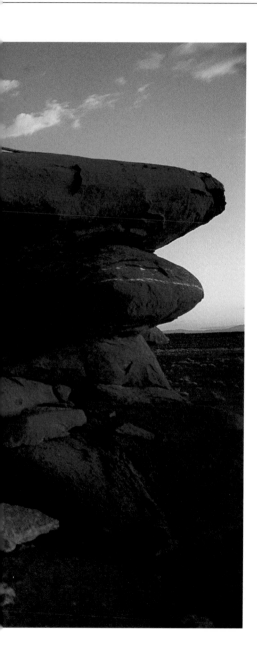

not to darken a blue sky, which creates an unnatural hue, but to remove the reflections that rob color from the vegetation. The reflections are caused by the waxy coating on leaves, blossoms, and fruit. If you make a habit of using a polarizer, your photographs will be characterized by strong, vibrant color.

Strive for technical perfection. If you have spent a lot of time, energy, and money getting to a scenic vista, it makes little sense not to use professional techniques. This means, among other things, attaining maximum sharpness by using a fine-grained film and a tripod, and bracketing shots so you can select the ideal exposure once the film is developed.

Make in-camera duplicates. It is better to make duplicates, if possible, in-camera rather than sending out an original for duping after the fact. In the publishing business, these are called 'similars'. They cost only 1/3 as much as the cheapest duplicates, and of course, they are better in quality. Multiple pictures of one scene allow you to submit the same photo simultaneously to more than one publisher. And the more the better; even a great image meets rejection most of the time, so play the odds.

Shoot verticals. I don't like to shoot verticals. It's unnatural. Human vision is based on a horizontal format due to the lateral arrangement of our eyes. Nevertheless, 90% of books and magazines are produced in a vertical shape because of the way a sheet of paper fits into a printing press.

Maligne Lake, Jasper National Park, Alberta. *Well known landmarks are good subjects for commercial landscape photographs. Most of them are, by definition, visually dramatic. In addition, they are needed for calendar and advertising layouts as characteristic symbols of a region. There is usually a good supply of such photographs, and those with dramatic skies are most often published. In many areas, attractive cloud formations occur in late summer when thunderstorms are common. Vertically composed images are also at a premium due to limited supply and high demand by magazines.*

Painted Desert, Arizona. *The red color of the rocks found in the southwestern United States is the result of iron-oxide deposits. In this image, these commercially valuable hues were strengthened by the warm light of sunset and a color enhancing filter.*

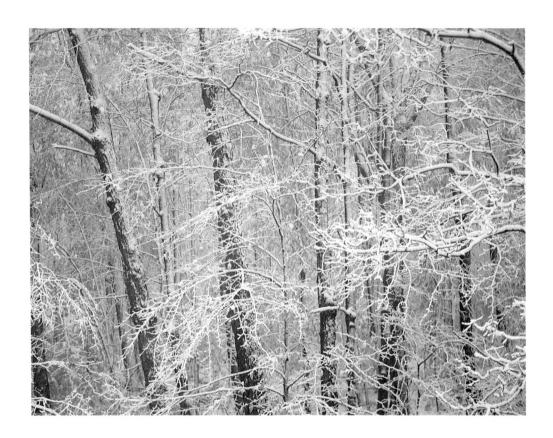

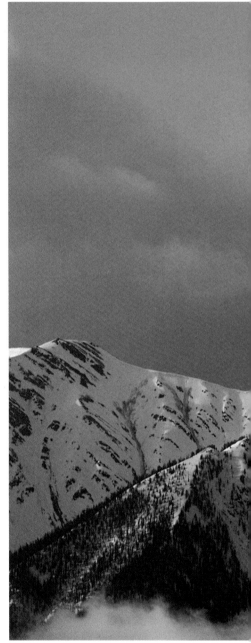

Beech and Maple Forest, Gatineau Park, Quebec. *This photograph was made with a 200 mm telephoto set at minimum aperture to achieve maximum depth-of-field. A warming filter (1a) was used to emphasize the orange leaves. I increased the exposure 1/2 stop over the meter reading to retain the clean white of the snow.*

Purcell Mountains, British Columbia. *Winter landscape photographs are more valuable than those shot at other times of the year. There is a strong demand for snowy scenics leading up to the Christmas holiday season, the busiest time of the year for advertising. In addition, there is a shortage of such pictures because photographers do most of their work in the warmer seasons.*

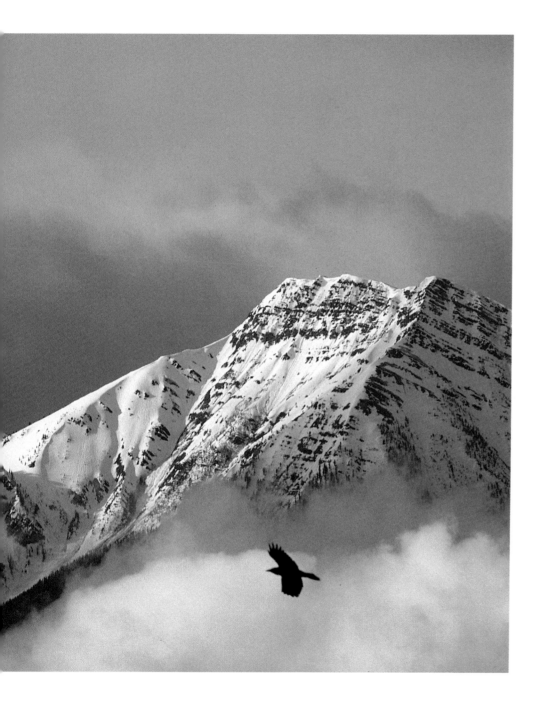

Consequently, these publications use a lot of vertical pictures, many of them full-page size, creating a big niche for upright photos.

Shoot Red. No color catches the eye more easily than red. As it happens, nature is mostly green and blue, so pictures with a red motif are rare and usually sit atop the pile of photos on an editor's desk.

Shoot in winter. Most magazines and calendars have a well defined seasonal appeal. They need pictures that clearly express spring, summer, fall, and winter. Every photographer shoots in the warmer seasons, but few do serious work in winter settings. Generally, if you have two similar photographs, one with snow, and one without, the former will sell twice as often.

Selling your photographs is almost as much fun as taking them. It's not the money, however, that makes it worthwhile. It's knowing that the image you worked hard to create has been recognized for its aesthetic value, and that its portrayal of wilderness communicates ideas of benefit to all life.

Appendix

B & H Photo-Video, 119 West 17th Street, New York, New York 10011, 1-800-947-9970. This is the mail order company of choice for professional photographers. Their prices are competitive, their service is reliable, and the sales staff are knowledgeable. I buy most of my equipment and film here. Call for a catalogue, or consult the back pages of *Popular Photography* magazine.

Leonard Lee Rue Enterprises, 138 Millbrook Road, Blairstown, New Jersey 07825, 1-908-362-5808. This company supplies a variety of specialized outdoor photography accessories (not cameras or lenses). It's a reliable source of Kimac individual slide protectors, which can be hard to find. They offer a wide variety of outdoor photography guides. Call or write for a catalogue.

Photo Traveler, Post Office Box 39912, Los Angeles, California 90039. This monthly newsletter, written by photographers, provides invaluable information on shooting logistics for scenic areas all over North America. I never leave on an expedition without taking along the relevant issues. Back issues are available covering many scenic hotspots.

Edward R. Byers Co., 29001 West Highway 58, Barstow, California 92311, 1-619-256-2377. This company supplies equatorial mounts for professional astrophotography for a variety of cameras.

SUGGESTED READING

American Landscape, David Muench, Graphic Arts Center Publishing, Portland, 1988

The Art of Nature, Photography by Brian W. Heinemann, Essays by Tim McNulty, Prior Publushing, Seattle, 1992.

The Creation, Ernst Haas, The Viking Press, New York, 1971.

Galen Rowell's Vision, Galen Rowell, Sierra Club Books, San Francisco, 1993.

Landscape Photography, The Art and Technique of Eight Modern Masters, edited by Don Earnest and Marisa Bulzone, Amphoto, New York, 1984.

Light on the Land, Art Wolfe, Beyond Words Publishing, Hillsboro, Oregon, 1991.

Photographer's Market Guide, (published yearly) Writer's Digest Books, Cincinnati, Ohio.

Photography & the Art of Seeing, Freeman Patterson, Sierra Club Books, San Francisco, 1990 (revised edition).

This Land of Europe, Dennis Stock, Kodansha International, New York, 1976.

PRODUCED BY TERRAPIN BOOKS
Santa Fe, New Mexico